Word Family Bingo Ladders

Fun-and-Easy Reproducible Games That Teach Kids the Top 25 Word Families

by Violet Findley

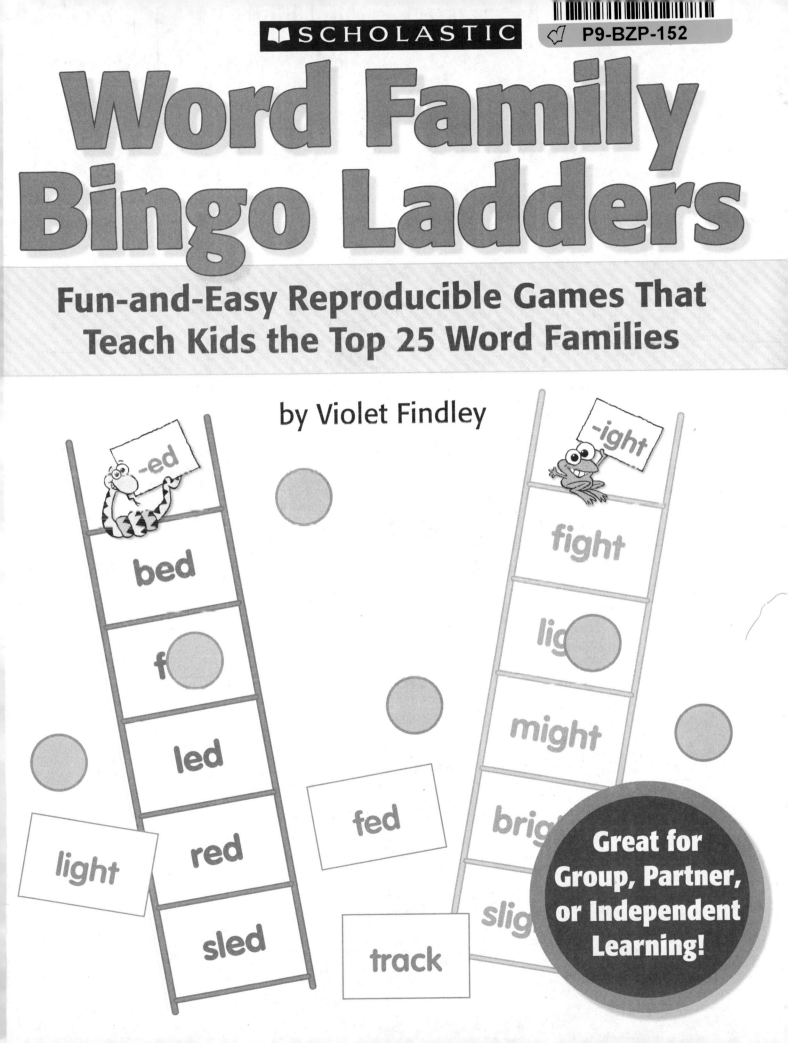

-ed

bed

f

led

red

sled

light

fed

track

-ight

fight

lig

might

brig

slig

Great for Group, Partner, or Independent Learning!

Written and conceived by Violet Findley
Cover and design by Brian LaRossa
Illustration by Doug Jones

ISBN-10: 0-545-09440-2/ ISBN-13: 978-0-545-09440-5

Contents

-ing

Introduction

Welcome to *Word Family Bingo Ladders*! Your students will learn how to play this engaging game in an instant. But the benefit of their playing it will last a lifetime.

That's because these charming bingo ladders teach the 25 word families that most frequently appear in print. And research shows that a knowledge of these word families helps lay the foundation for long-term reading success. Why? When children have repeated encounters with word families—also known as *phonograms*—they come to recognize spelling patterns, gaining the ability to decode member words by analogy. Thus, when children internalize the pronunciation of the phonogram *–ack*, they can easily master all of the members of the -ack family, including *back*, *hack*, *sack*, *crack*, and *knack*. The ability to decode by analogy is an empowering tool because it enables children to read hundreds and hundreds of words automatically. And that "automaticity" leads to reading confidence and—our ultimate goal for students—fluency.

A few minutes a day or week is all it takes to integrate word family instruction into your school day. And incorporating these lively bingo ladders into your routine is the perfect way to do just that. Treat the whole class to a quick game just before the bell rings. Or place laminated sets in a learning center for small groups or pairs to play independently. Make bingo ladders a classroom habit—and watch your students' reading skills soar!

Featured Word Families

The bingo games in this book teach these top 25 word families:

-ack, -ail, -ake, -an, -ank, -ap, -at, -ate, -eat, -ell, -est, -y, -ick, -ight, -ill, -ine, -ing, -ink, -ip, -ock, -ore, -ot, -uck, -ug, -ump

Connection to the McREL Language Arts Standards

The bingo games in this book are designed to support you in meeting these essential K–2 standards.

✓ Uses basic elements of phonetic analysis (e.g. common letter/sound relationships, beginning and ending consonants, vowel sounds, blends, word patterns) to decode unknown words

✓ Uses basic elements of structural analysis such as spelling patterns to decode unknown words

Source: *Content Knowledge: A Compendium of Standards and Benchmarks for PreK–12 Education*, (4th edition). (Mid-Continent Regional Educational Laboratory, 2004)

Preparing the Games for Play

To make each of the 25 bingo games, follow these simple directions:

1. Choose the word family you want to teach. Make a photocopy of the three-page game set, which includes a word chart, word cards, and six word family ladders. For added durability, copy the set onto card stock. (Tip: For whole-class play, make duplicate copies of the ladders so that every child gets one.)

2. Cut the bingo ladders and word cards apart along the dashed lines.

3. Optional: Color the ladders to make them extra appealing. Laminate the ladders to make them extra strong.

4. Purchase or prepare markers for the game, such as plastic disks, dried beans, buttons, or the reproducible markers on page 91. Also, prepare a brown bag or box with the name of the word family written on it.

5. Store each word family game in a labeled manila envelope.

Components

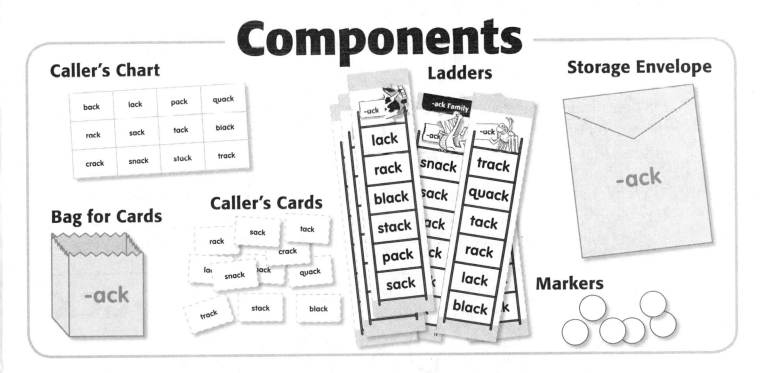

Caller's Chart

back	lack	pack	quack
rack	sack	tack	black
crack	snack	stack	track

Bag for Cards

-ack

Caller's Cards

rack sack tack
crack
la snack ack quack
track stack black

Ladders

-ack

lack
rack
black
stack
pack
sack

snack
sack
ack
ck
ck
k

-ack Family

-ack

track
quack
tack
rack
lack
black k

-ack

Storage Envelope

-ack

Markers

How to Play

The games in this book can be played by the whole class, small groups, or pairs. Here are easy instructions:

1. Choose the word family game you want to play, such as -*at*. (Tip: You can also use the blank templates on pages 86–90 to teach a word family not included in this book.)

2. Make multiple copies of the word family ladders and distribute one to each student.

3. Give each student six markers.

4. Invite a student volunteer to act as the caller (or do so yourself). Provide the caller with the word family chart and a brown bag or box filled with the cut-apart word family words.

5. Ask the caller to pull out a word family card (such as *bat*), read it aloud, and place it on the word family chart.

6. When a word appears on a student's board, he/she should cover it with a marker.

7. Play continues with the caller reading aloud each word and students covering the words with markers. When a student has covered all six words on his/her ladder, that student shouts, "Word Family Bingo!"

8. The caller should check the student's board to make sure that he/she is in fact a winner. If so, lead students in a round of applause. (NOTE: If you are playing with multiples copies of the same bingo board, there will be multiple winners.)

Word Family Activities to Extend Learning

Super Silly Sentence

Choose a phonogram such as *–at*. With students, brainstorm a long list of rhyming words (*flat, mat, that, sat, rat, cat, hat, fat*). Write them on the board or cards that can be reordered on the chalk tray. Next, challenge children to work together to make up a sentence that includes as many of the words as possible; for example: *The fat cat that sat on the mat wanted to wear the flat hat of a rat.* Don't be afraid to get super silly! For added fun, ask volunteers to illustrate one or more of the silly sentences.

Beanbag Rhyme Toss

Support kinesthetic learners with this engaging rhyming game! Invite students to stand in a circle and toss a beanbag around. Start them off with a word containing a phonogram that is easy to rhyme, such as *bug*. Ask the child holding the beanbag to name a rhyming word (for example, *hug*) and then toss the beanbag to the student to his or her right, then have that student do the same. If a child cannot name a new rhyming word, he or she says "pass" and hands—not tosses—the beanbag to the next child. When three kids in a row say "pass," it's time to start a new game with a fresh phonogram.

Collaborative Word Family Dictionaries

Enrich learning by publishing a class set of word family dictionaries. Divide the class into groups, and assign each a different phonogram (*-ack, -ick, -uck,* and so on). Challenge each group of bookmakers to work together to write a new rhyming word on each page (*back, sack, tack, shack, track*) and to illustrate them with simple pictures and then label the cover (for example, "Our *–ACT* Words"). When the dictionaries are complete, place them in an accessible spot for kids to turn to for friendly reading, writing, and spelling support.

Rhyme Time Concentration

Using two or more phonogram lists for reference, jot rhyming words on index cards—one word for each card. (Make sure you include an even number of rhyming words for each family.) Shuffle the cards, then place them face down in rows. Invite children to take turns turning over the cards to make matches. If two words rhyme (such as *ban* and *van*), the student gets to keep the cards and try again. Play continues until all the cards have been picked up. The child with the most cards wins.

Word Family Fish

Make a class set of about 36 playing cards, using several rhyming word pairs. (Tip: You can purchase blank playing cards at many teacher stores.) Tell children that they will be using the cards to play Word Family Fish. The rules of the game are the same as the classic Go Fish, except children will be looking for sets of rhyming words instead of number/face cards. The child with the most matches wins!

I Spy Riddles

Play a rhyming word version of I Spy using items in your classroom. For example, "I spy with my little eye, something you read that rhymes with *look*." (*book*) Or "I spy with my little eye, something you write with that rhymes with *Ken*. (*pen*) Once children have mastered the concept, invite them to generate their own riddles to share with classmates.

Rhyming Relay Race

Divide the class into three or four teams, and have each line up. On the board, write a different word for each team—for example, *cake, king, duck.* (Tip: Make sure you select phonograms with plenty of rhyming word possibilities.) Next, challenge each child, in turn, to come up to the board and add a rhyming word to his or her team's list. Team members can help each other out. The team to generate the longest list is the winner!

Word Family Bingo Ladders

-ock

-ug

-ight

CALLER'S CHART

back	lack	pack	quack
rack	sack	tack	black
crack	snack	stack	track

CALLER'S CARDS

back	lack	pack	quack
rack	sack	tack	black
crack	snack	stack	track

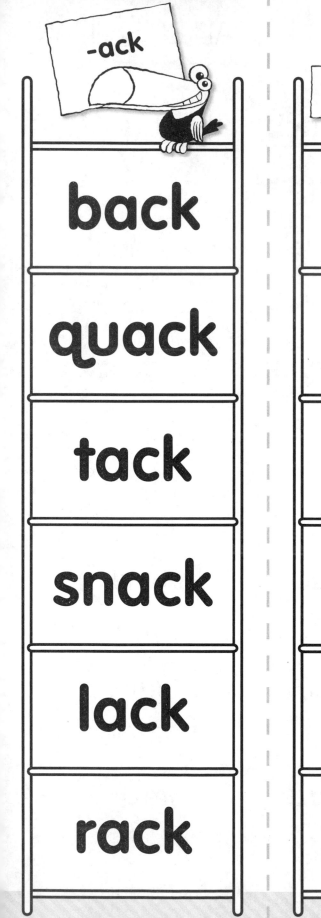

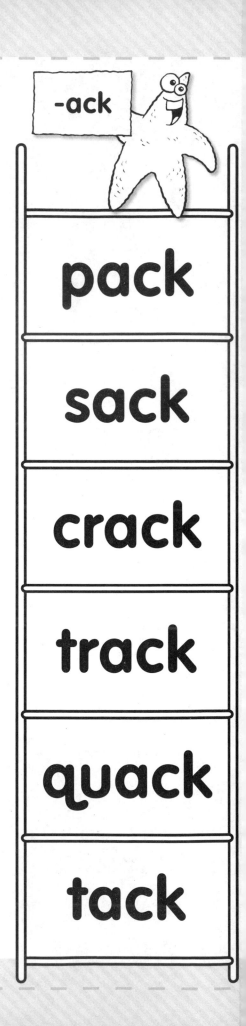

back	lack	pack
quack	rack	sack
tack	black	crack
snack	stack	track
lack	pack	quack
rack	sack	tack

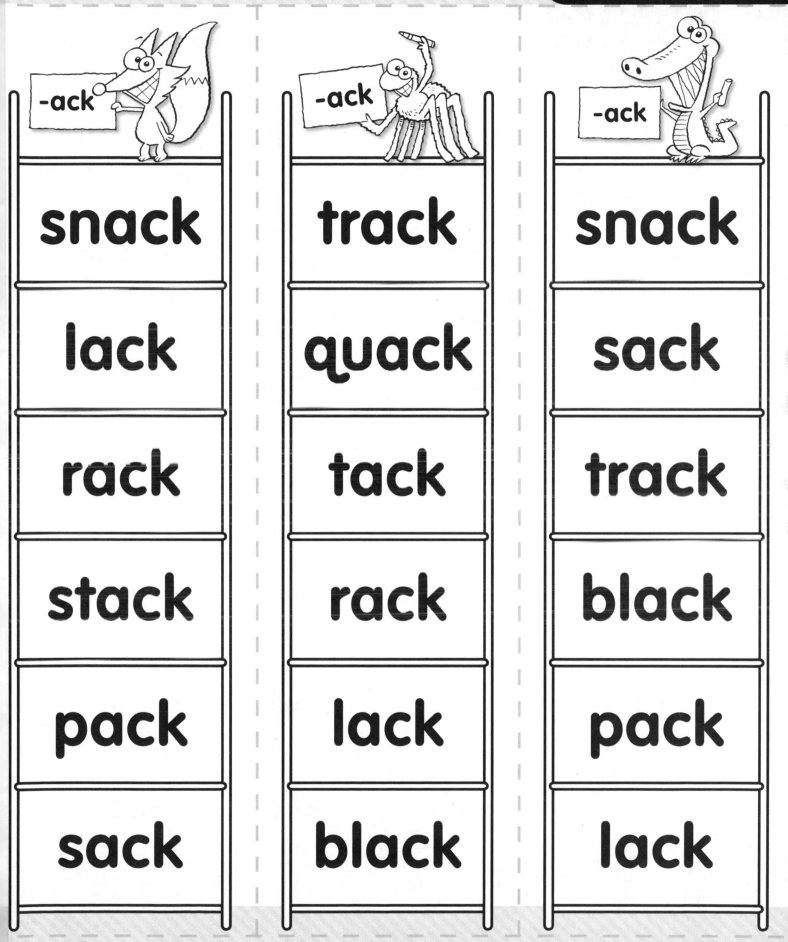

-ack	-ack	-ack
snack	track	snack
lack	quack	sack
rack	tack	track
stack	rack	black
pack	lack	pack
sack	black	lack

CALLER'S CHART

bail	fail	hail	jail
nail	pail	quail	rail
sail	tail	snail	trail

CALLER'S CARDS

bail	fail	hail	jail
nail	pail	quail	rail
sail	tail	snail	trail

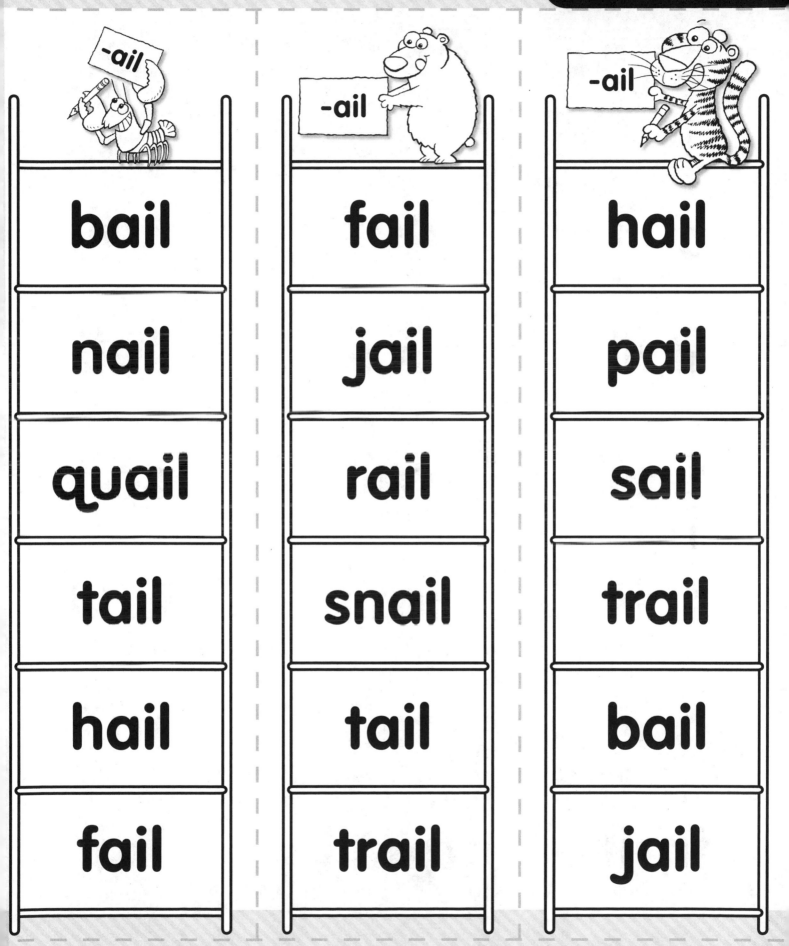

bail	fail	hail
nail	jail	pail
quail	rail	sail
tail	snail	trail
hail	tail	bail
fail	trail	jail

LADDERS

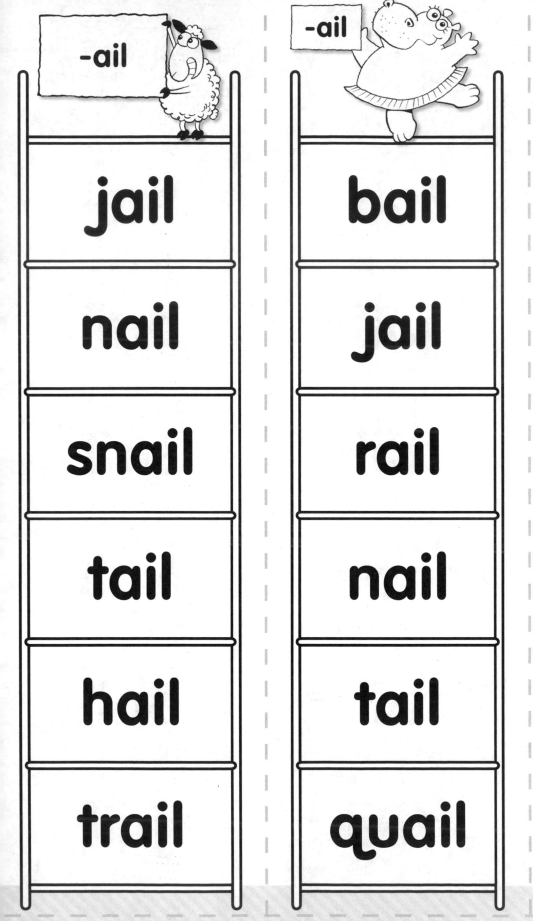

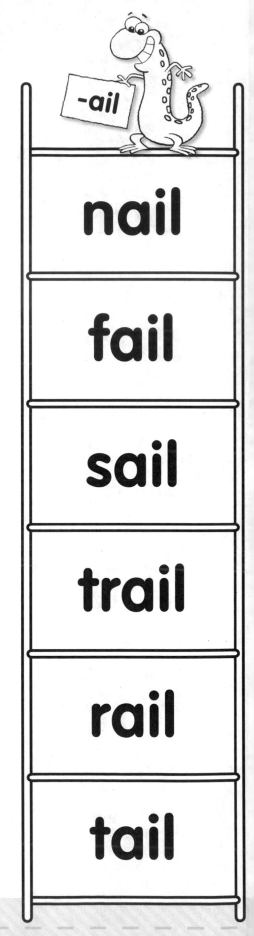

-ail

jail	bail	nail
nail	jail	fail
snail	rail	sail
tail	nail	trail
hail	tail	rail
trail	quail	tail

CALLER'S CHART

bake	cake	fake	lake
make	rake	take	wake
brake	flake	shake	snake

CALLER'S CARDS

bake	cake	fake	lake
make	rake	take	wake
brake	flake	shake	snake

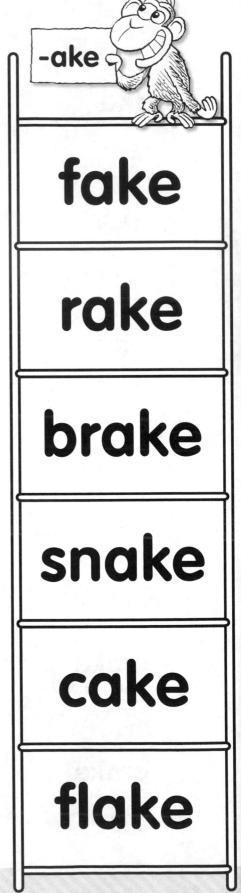

bake	cake	fake
lake	make	rake
take	wake	brake
flake	shake	snake
snake	bake	cake
cake	snake	flake

-ake Family

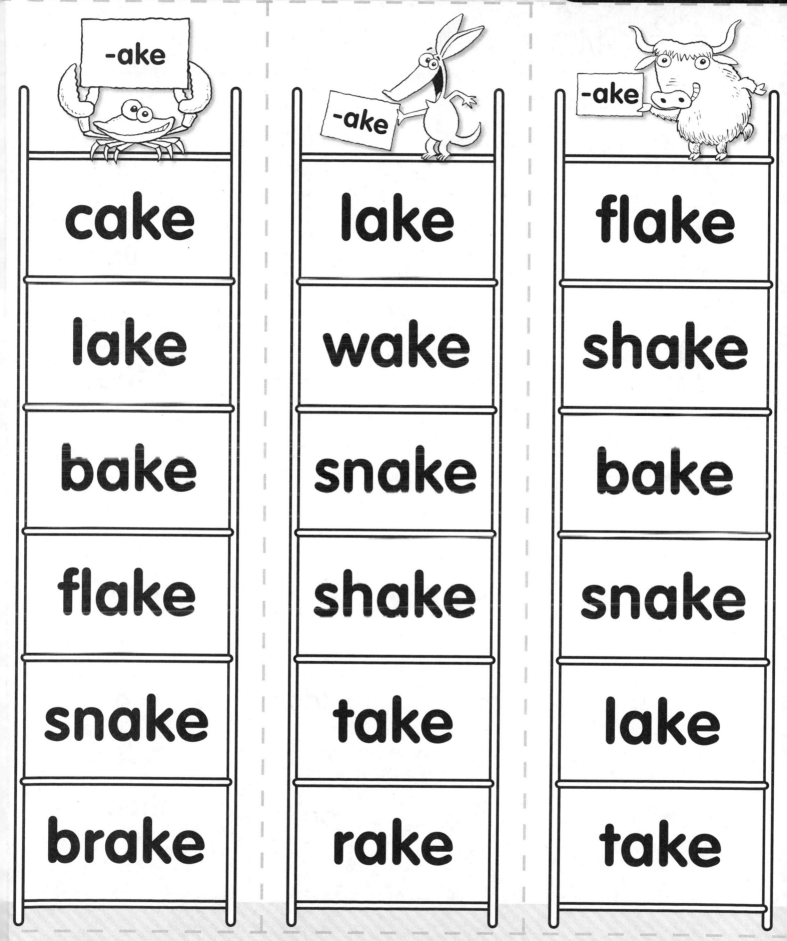

-ake	-ake	-ake
cake	lake	flake
lake	wake	shake
bake	snake	bake
flake	shake	snake
snake	take	lake
brake	rake	take

CALLER'S CHART

ban	can	fan	man
pan	ran	tan	van
clan	plan	span	than

CALLER'S CARDS

ban	can	fan	man
pan	ran	tan	van
clan	plan	span	than

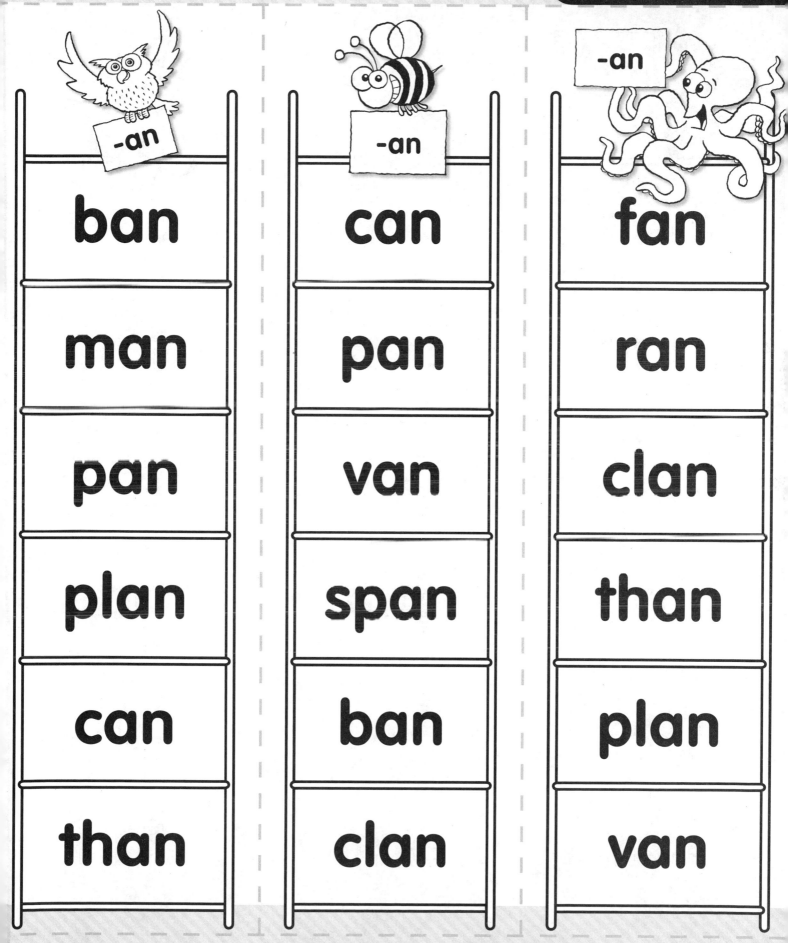

ban	can	fan
man	pan	ran
pan	van	clan
plan	span	than
can	ban	plan
than	clan	van

-an Family   LADDERS

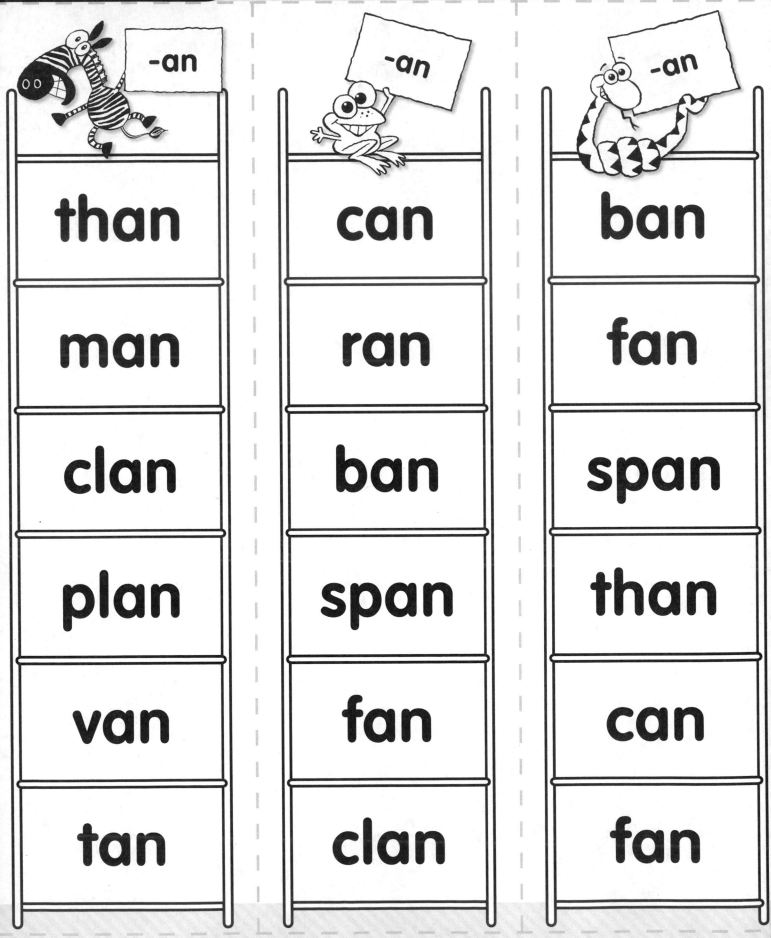

-an	-an	-an
than	can	ban
man	ran	fan
clan	ban	span
plan	span	than
van	fan	can
tan	clan	fan

CALLER'S CHART

bank	**sank**	**tank**	**yank**
blank	**clank**	**crank**	**drank**
flank	**plank**	**prank**	**thank**

CALLER'S CARDS

bank	sank	tank	yank
blank	clank	crank	drank
flank	plank	prank	thank

LADDERS

bank	sank	tank
yank	blank	crank
crank	drank	flank
plank	prank	thank
tank	bank	yank
drank	flank	prank

-ank	-ank	-ank
prank	bank	drank
thank	blank	tank
sank	plank	crank
plank	thank	blank
tank	bank	yank
bank	sank	tank

CALLER'S CHART

cap	gap	lap	map
nap	rap	sap	tap
clap	snap	trap	wrap

CALLER'S CARDS

cap	gap	lap	map
nap	rap	sap	tap
clap	snap	trap	wrap

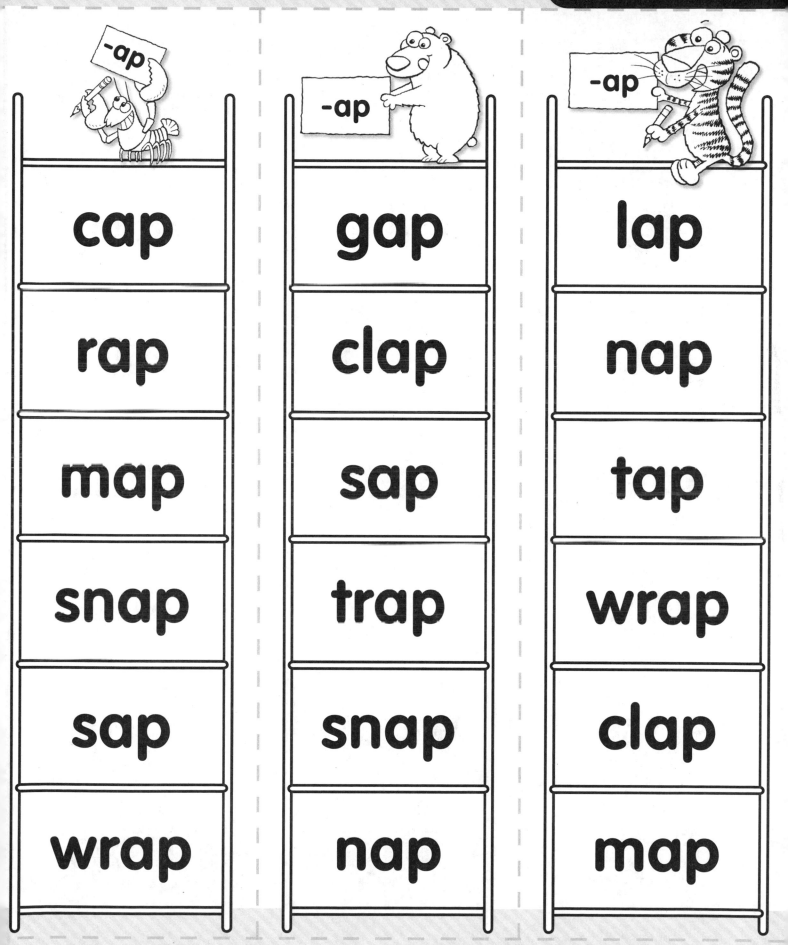

cap	gap	lap
rap	clap	nap
map	sap	tap
snap	trap	wrap
sap	snap	clap
wrap	nap	map

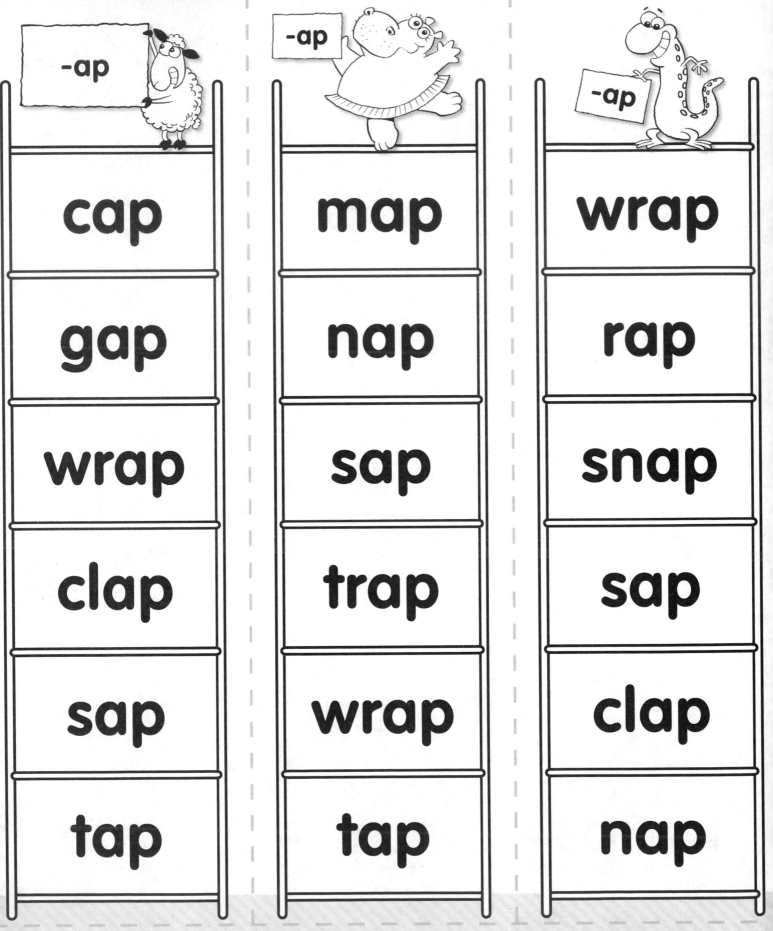

cap	map	wrap
gap	nap	rap
wrap	sap	snap
clap	trap	sap
sap	wrap	clap
tap	tap	nap

CALLER'S CHART

bat	cat	fat	pat
rat	sat	vat	brat
chat	flat	slat	that

CALLER'S CARDS

bat	cat	fat	pat
rat	sat	vat	brat
chat	flat	slat	that

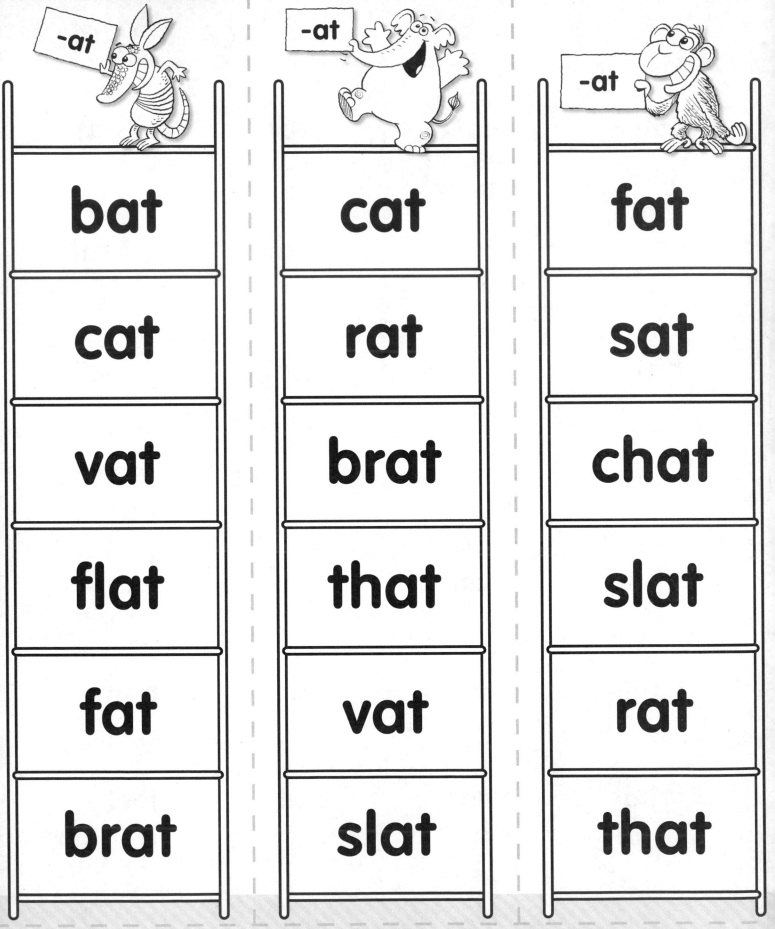

bat	cat	fat
cat	rat	sat
vat	brat	chat
flat	that	slat
fat	vat	rat
brat	slat	that

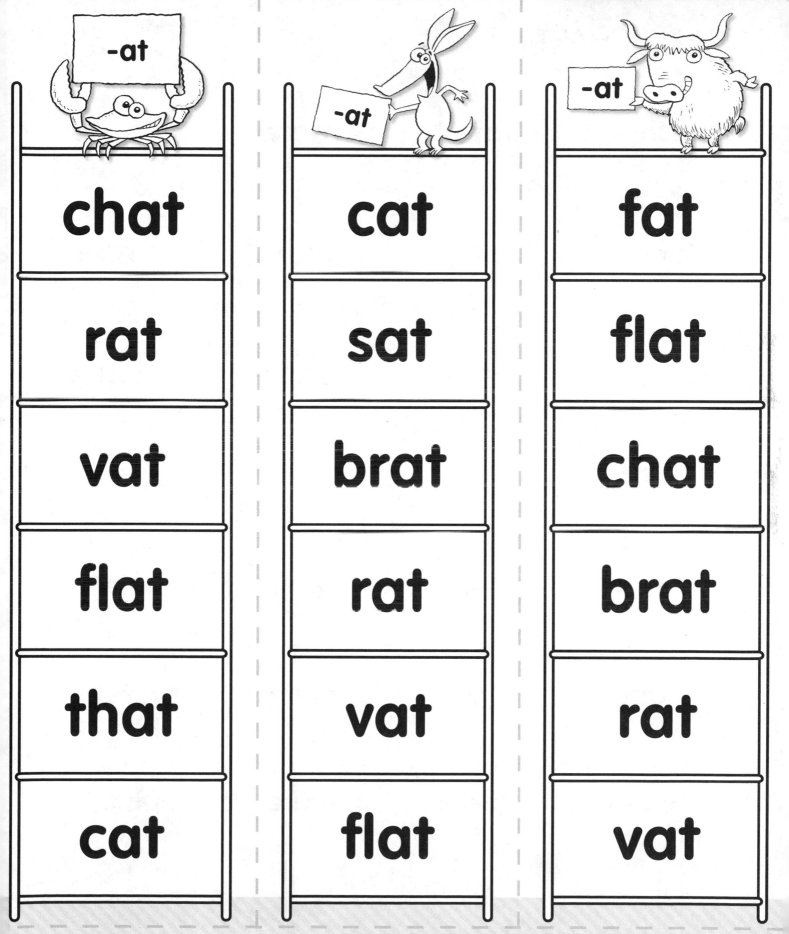

-at

chat

rat

vat

flat

that

cat

-at

cat

sat

brat

rat

vat

flat

-at

fat

flat

chat

brat

rat

vat

CALLER'S CHART

date	fate	gate	hate
Kate	late	mate	rate
crate	plate	skate	state

CALLER'S CARDS

date	fate	gate	hate
Kate	late	mate	rate
crate	plate	skate	state

-ate Family

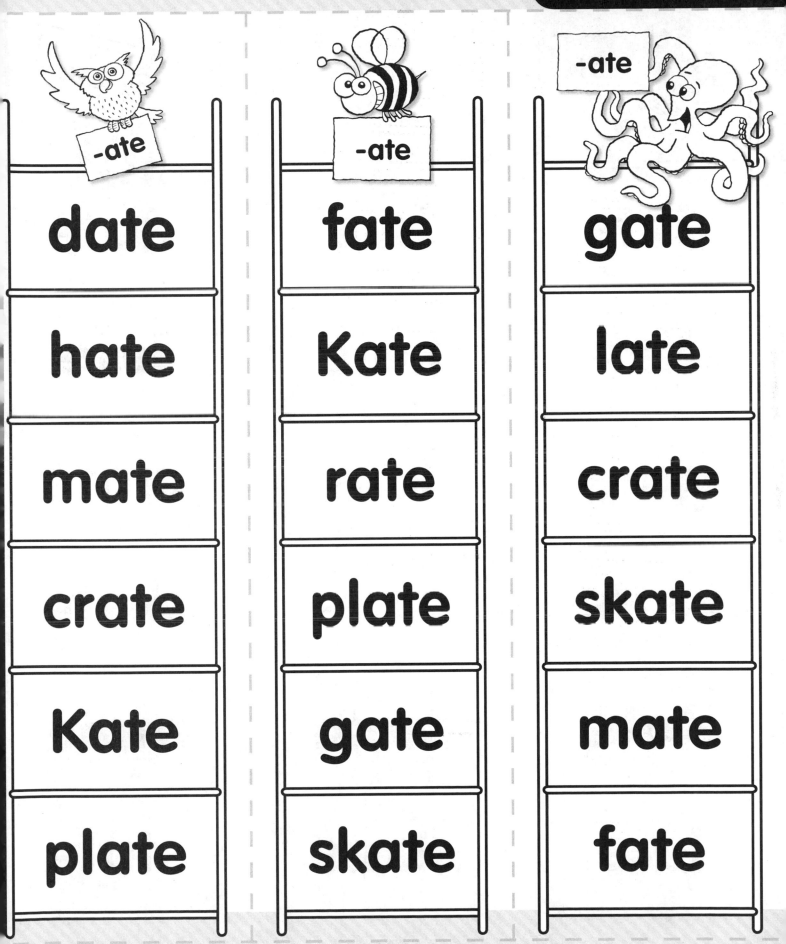

-ate	-ate	-ate
date	fate	gate
hate	Kate	late
mate	rate	crate
crate	plate	skate
Kate	gate	mate
plate	skate	fate

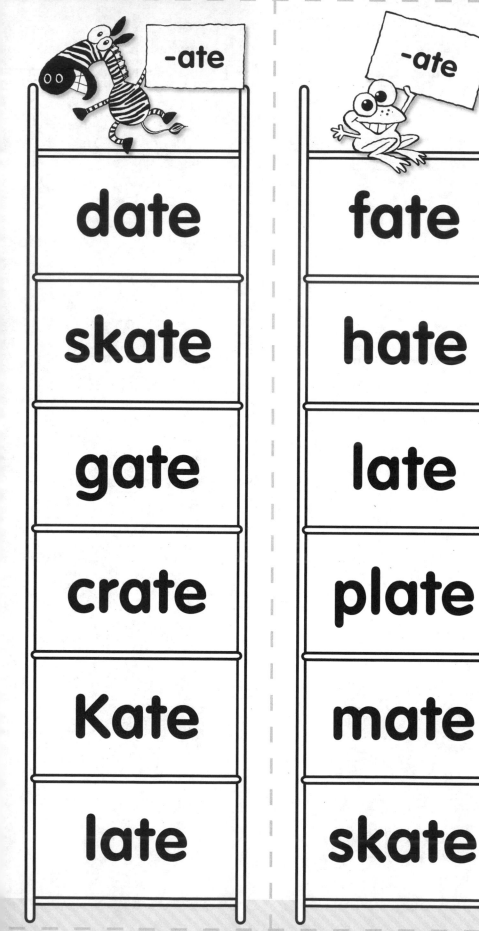

date	fate	gate
skate	hate	late
gate	late	crate
crate	plate	skate
Kate	mate	mate
late	skate	state

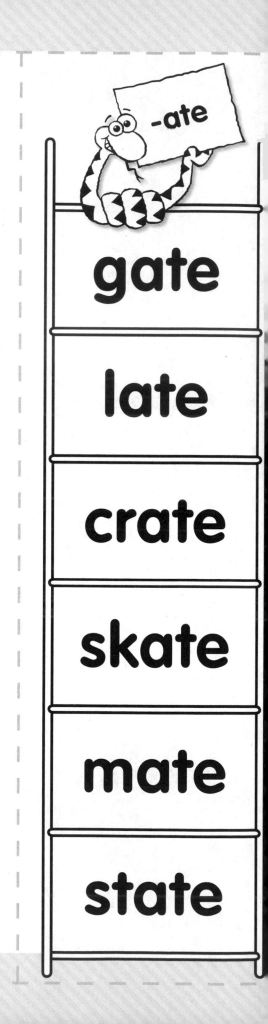

CALLER'S CHART

beat	feat	heat	meat
neat	seat	bleat	cheat
cleat	pleat	treat	wheat

CALLER'S CARDS

beat	feat	heat	meat
neat	seat	bleat	cheat
cleat	pleat	treat	wheat

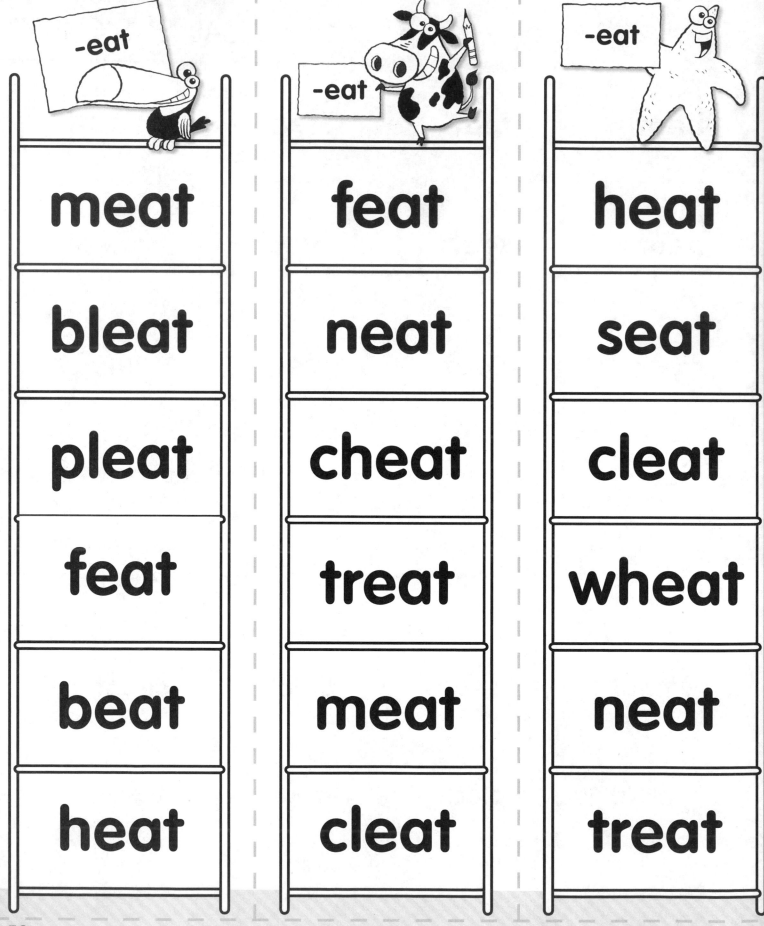

-eat	-eat	-eat
meat	feat	heat
bleat	neat	seat
pleat	cheat	cleat
feat	treat	wheat
beat	meat	neat
heat	cleat	treat

-eat Family

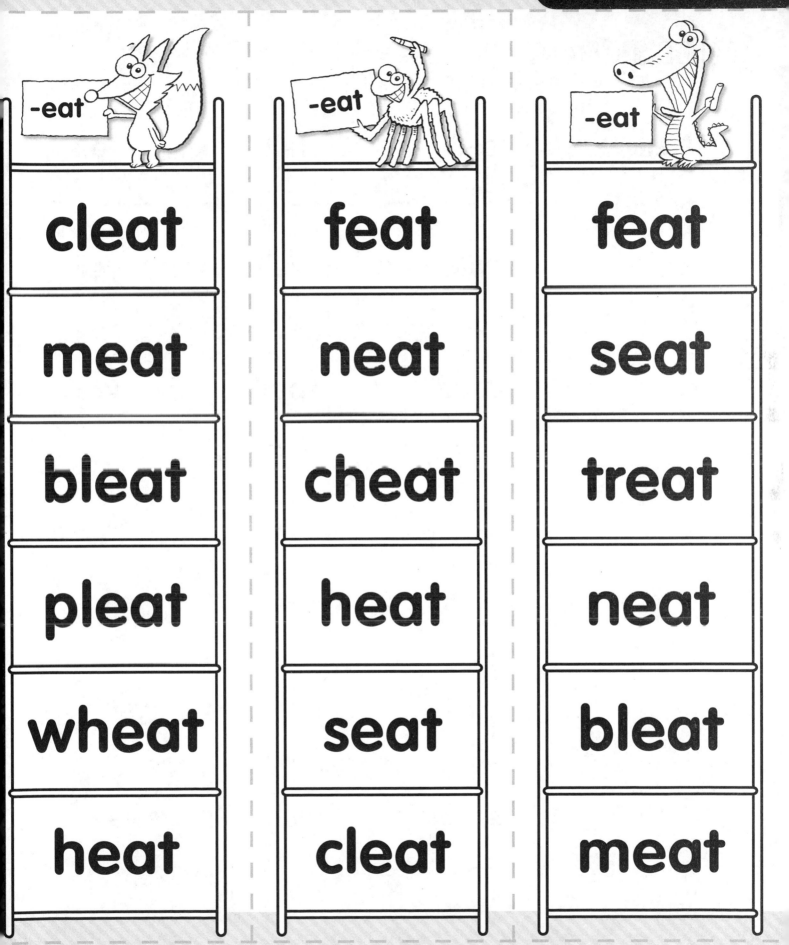

-eat	-eat	-eat
cleat	feat	feat
meat	neat	seat
bleat	cheat	treat
pleat	heat	neat
wheat	seat	bleat
heat	cleat	meat

-ell Family

CALLER'S CHART

bell	cell	fell	jell
sell	tell	well	yell
shell	smell	spell	swell

CALLER'S CARDS

bell	cell	fell	jell
sell	tell	well	yell
shell	smell	spell	swell

-ell

-ell

-ell

bell	cell	fell
jell	sell	tell
well	yell	shell
smell	spell	swell
shell	well	bell
swell	smell	spell

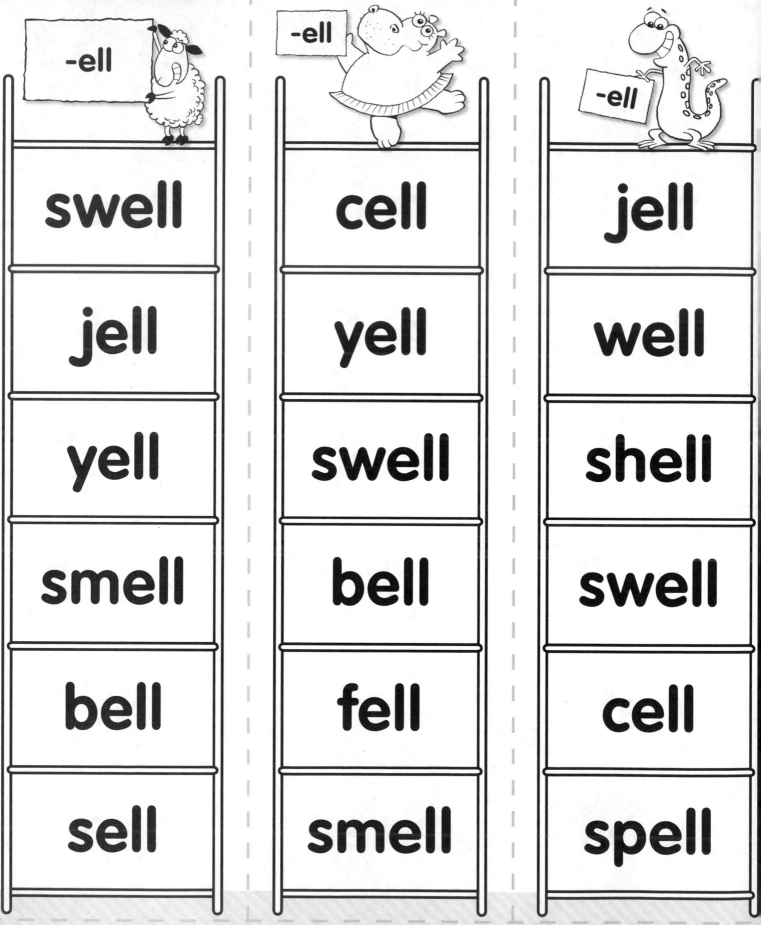

-ell	-ell	-ell
swell	cell	jell
jell	yell	well
yell	swell	shell
smell	bell	swell
bell	fell	cell
sell	smell	spell

CALLER'S CHART

best	jest	lest	nest
pest	test	vest	west
zest	chest	crest	quest

CALLER'S CARDS

best	jest	lest	nest
pest	test	vest	west
zest	chest	crest	quest

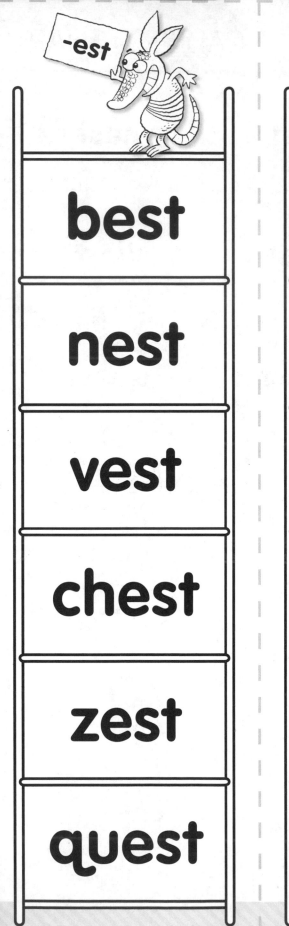

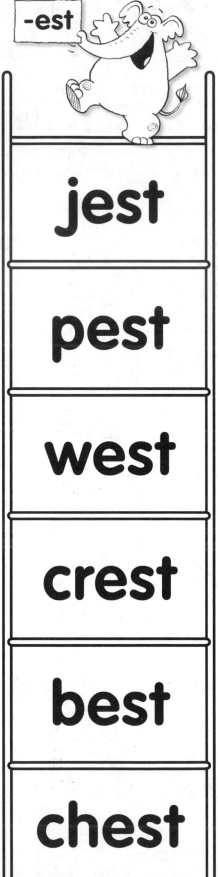

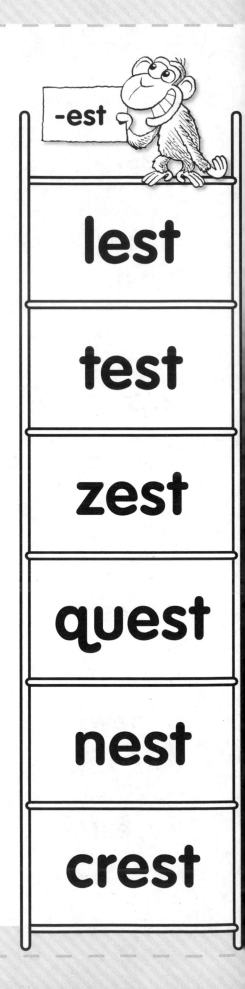

best	jest	lest
nest	pest	test
vest	west	zest
chest	crest	quest
zest	best	nest
quest	chest	crest

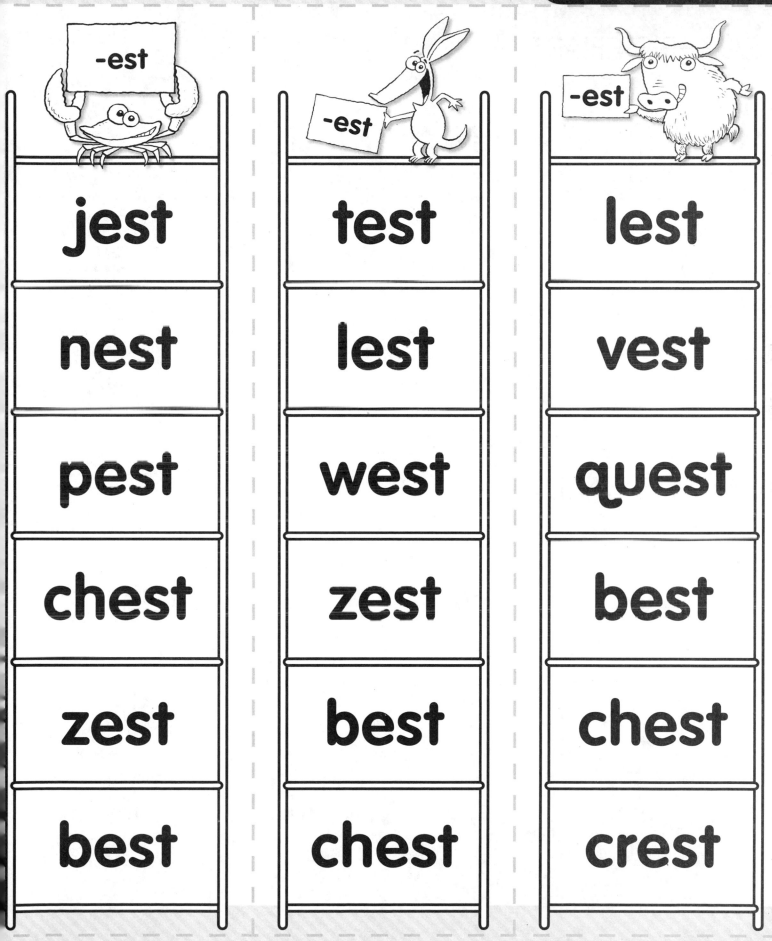

jest
nest
pest
chest
zest
best

test
lest
west
zest
best
chest

lest
vest
quest
best
chest
crest

43

CALLER'S CHART

by	my	cry	dry
fly	fry	pry	shy
sky	spy	try	why

CALLER'S CARDS

by	my	cry	dry
fly	fry	pry	shy
sky	spy	try	why

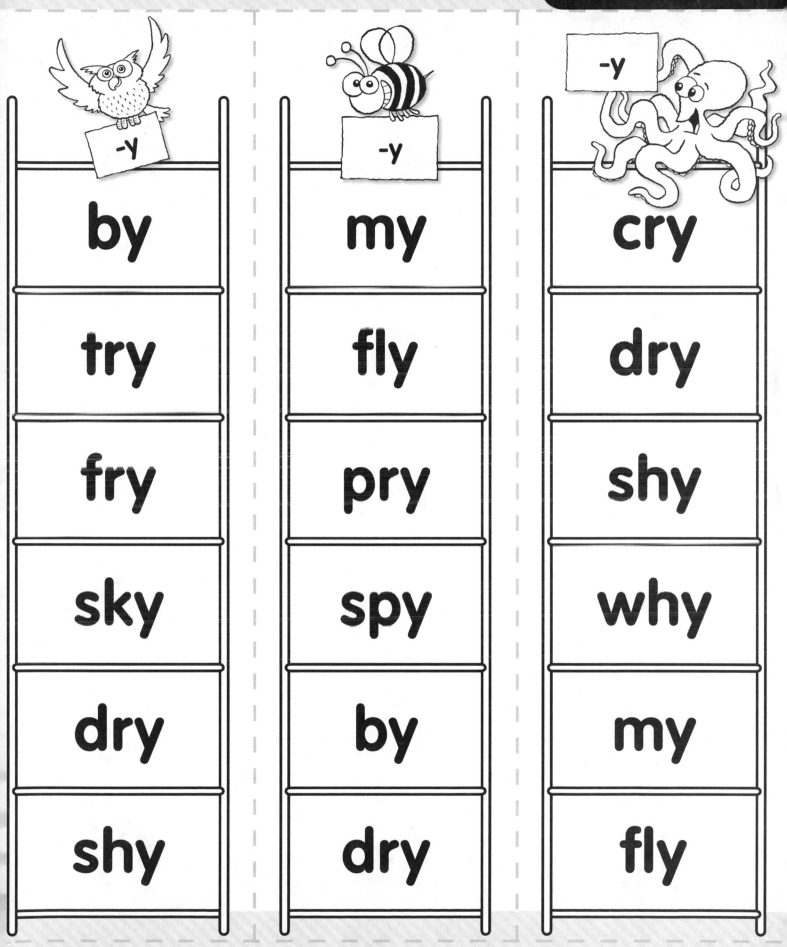

by	my	cry
try	fly	dry
fry	pry	shy
sky	spy	why
dry	by	my
shy	dry	fly

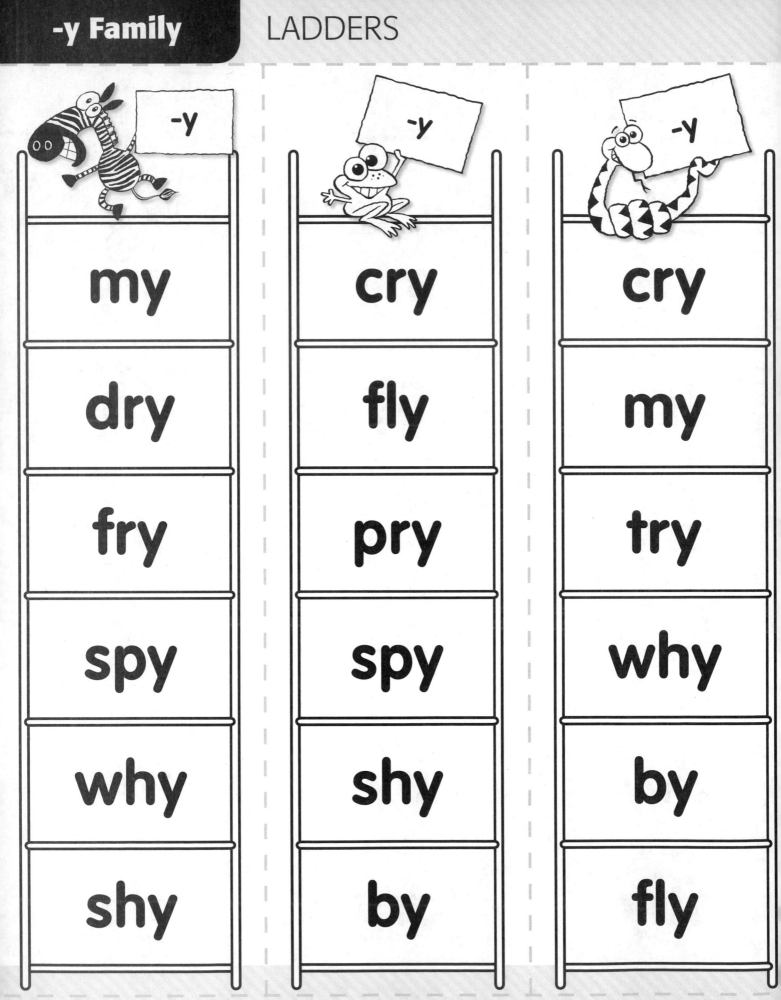

my	cry	cry
dry	fly	my
fry	pry	try
spy	spy	why
why	shy	by
shy	by	fly

CALLER'S CHART

kick	lick	pick	quick
sick	tick	chick	click
slick	stick	thick	trick

CALLER'S CARDS

kick	lick	pick	quick
sick	tick	chick	click
slick	stick	thick	trick

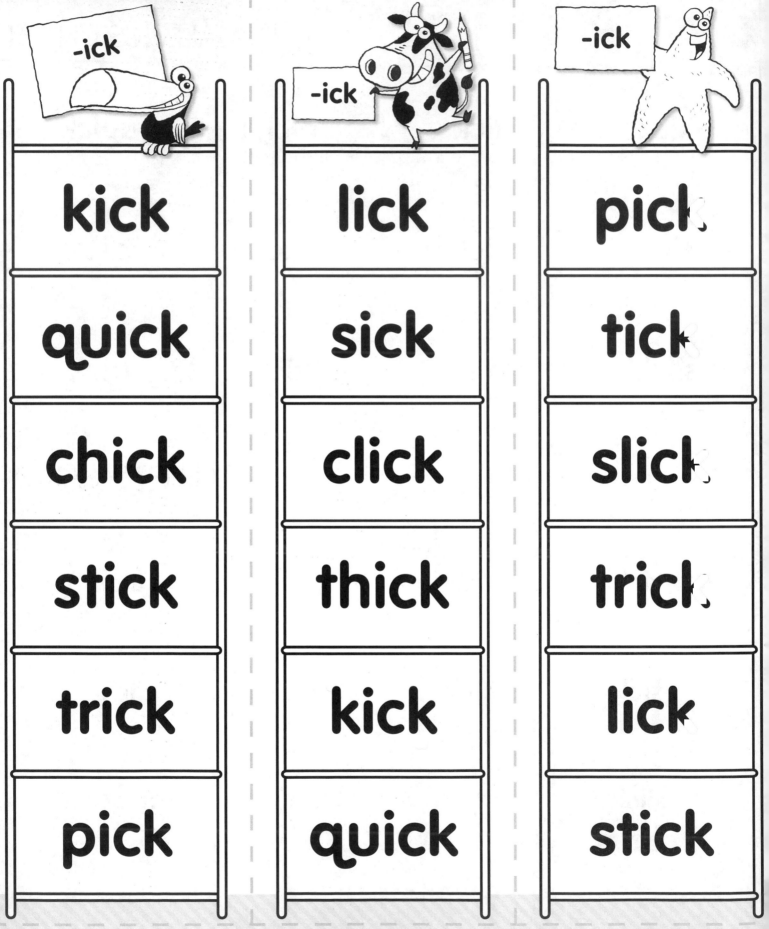

-ick

-ick

-ick

kick	lick	pick
quick	sick	tick
chick	click	slick
stick	thick	trick
trick	kick	lick
pick	quick	stick

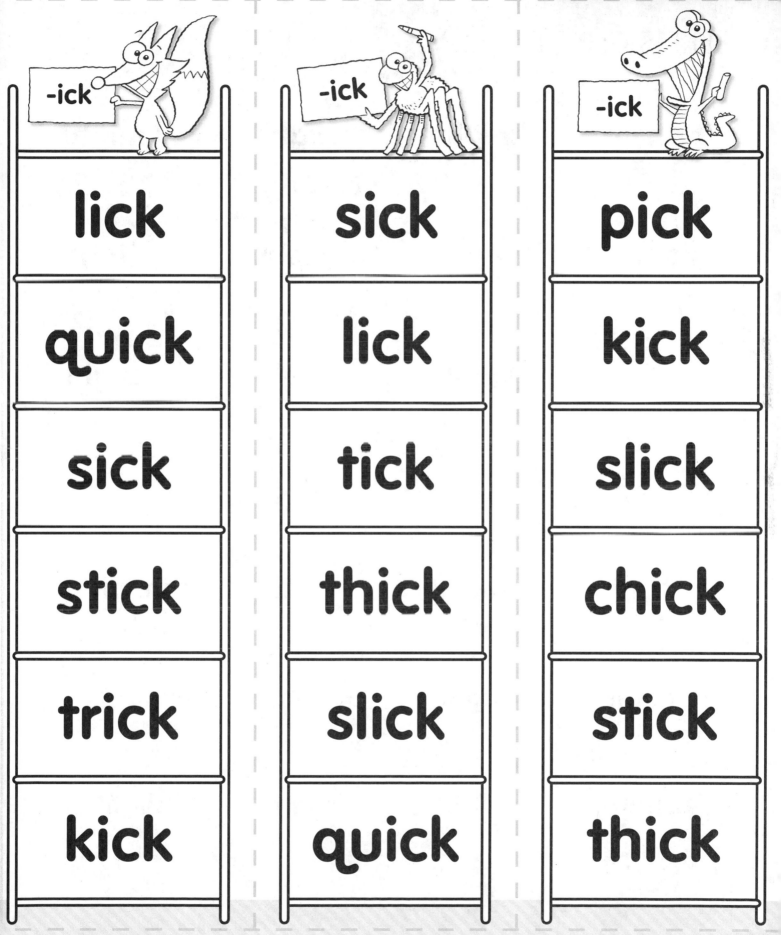

-ick	-ick	-ick
lick	sick	pick
quick	lick	kick
sick	tick	slick
stick	thick	chick
trick	slick	stick
kick	quick	thick

CALLER'S CHART

fight	knight	light	might
night	right	sight	tight
bright	flight	fright	slight

CALLER'S CARDS

fight	knight	light	might
night	right	sight	tight
bright	flight	fright	slight

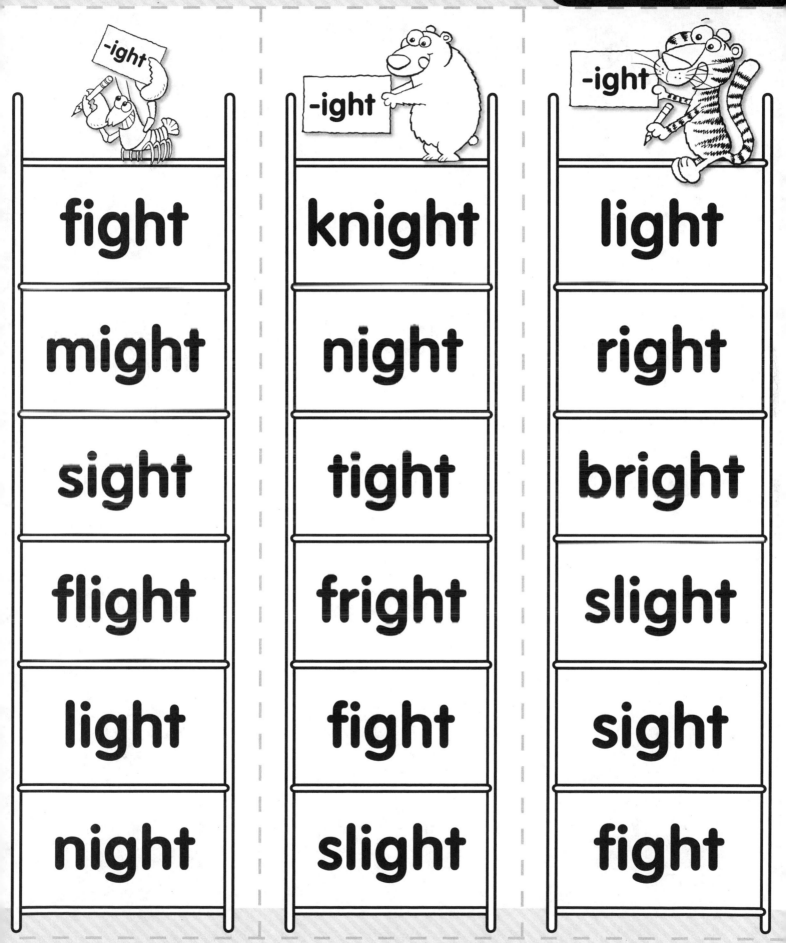

fight	knight	light
might	night	right
sight	tight	bright
flight	fright	slight
light	fight	sight
night	slight	fight

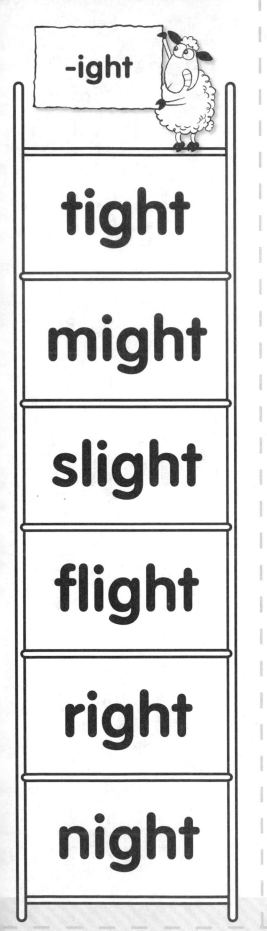

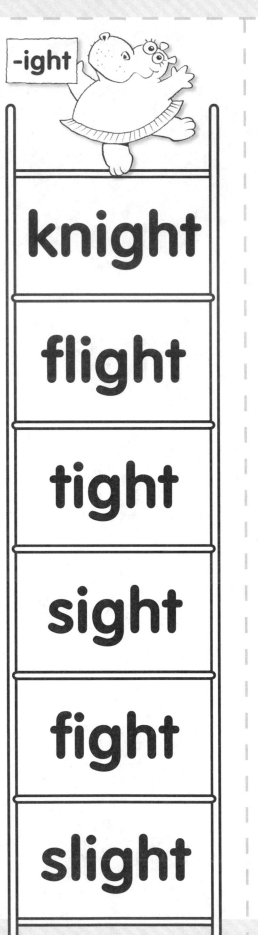

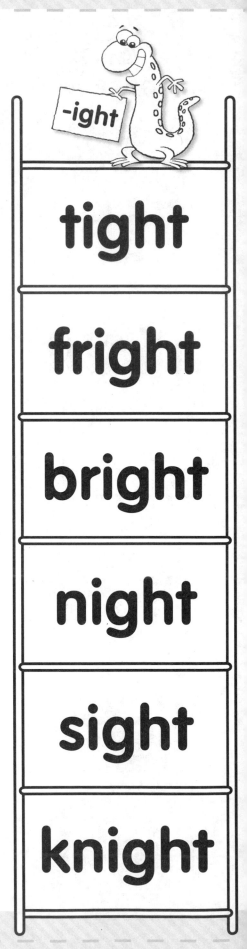

tight	knight	tight
might	flight	fright
slight	tight	bright
flight	sight	night
right	fight	sight
night	slight	knight

CALLER'S CHART

fill	gill	mill	sill
will	chill	drill	grill
skill	spill	still	thrill

CALLER'S CARDS

fill	gill	mill	sill
will	chill	drill	grill
skill	spill	still	thrill

LADDERS

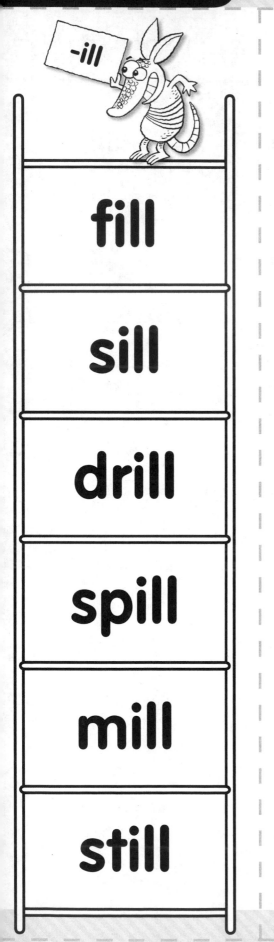

fill
sill
drill
spill
mill
still

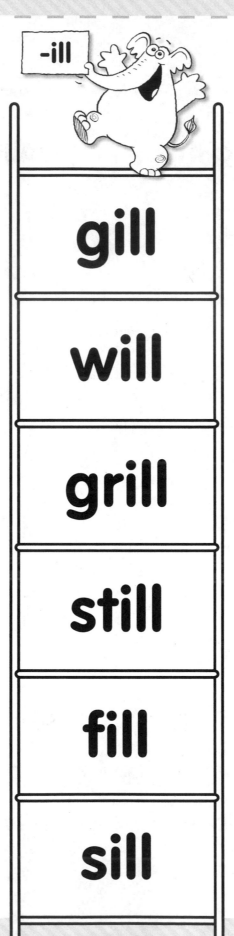

gill
will
grill
still
fill
sill

mill
chill
skill
thrill
drill
will

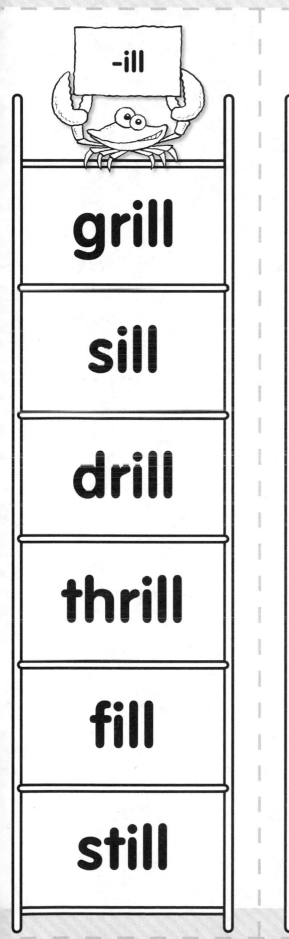

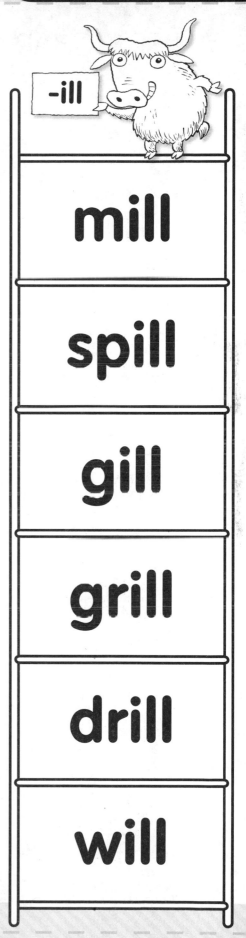

grill	drill	mill
sill	will	spill
drill	grill	gill
thrill	still	grill
fill	fill	drill
still	chill	will

CALLER'S CHART

dine	fine	line	mine
nine	pine	vine	shine
shrine	spine	swine	whine

CALLER'S CARDS

dine	fine	line	mine
nine	pine	vine	shine
shrine	spine	swine	whine

-ine Family

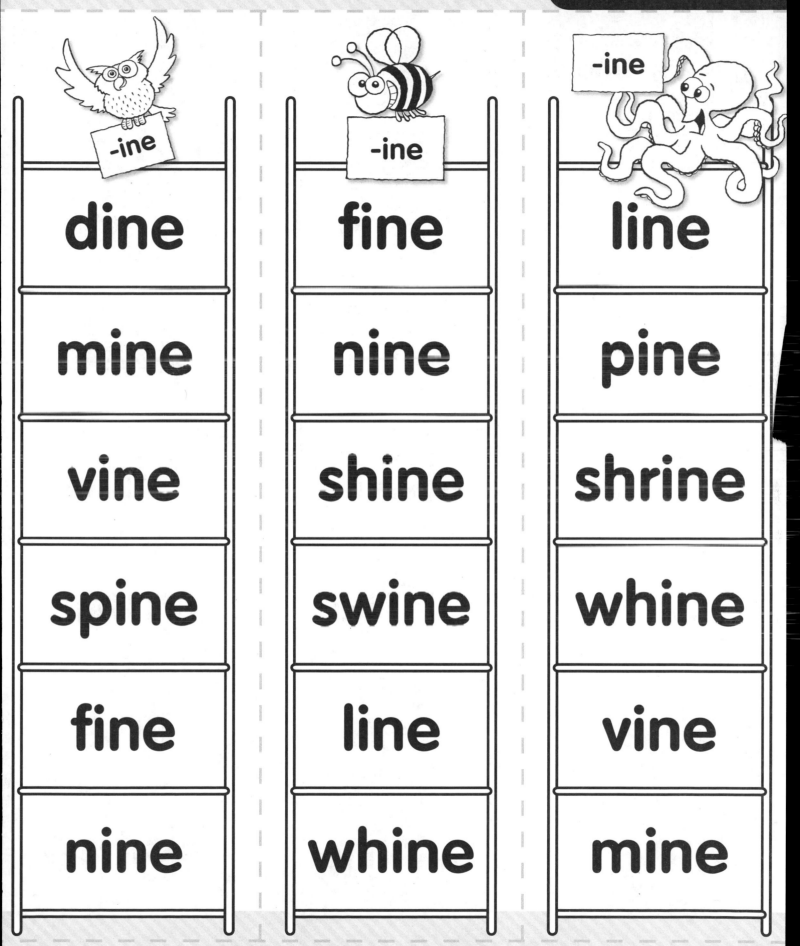

dine	fine	line
mine	nine	pine
vine	shine	shrine
spine	swine	whine
fine	line	vine
nine	whine	mine

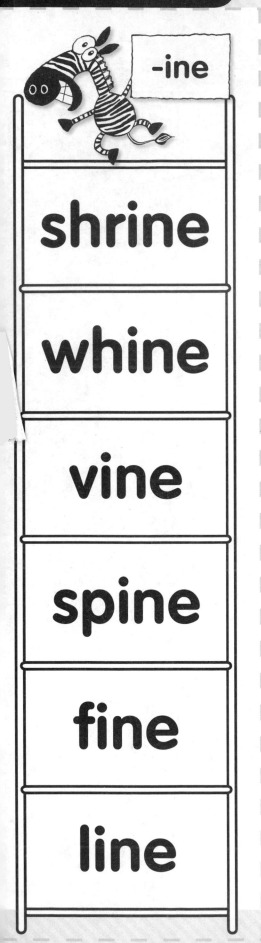

shrine

whine

vine

spine

fine

line

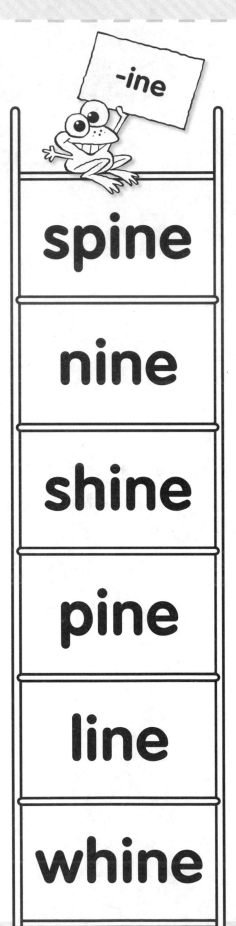

spine

nine

shine

pine

line

whine

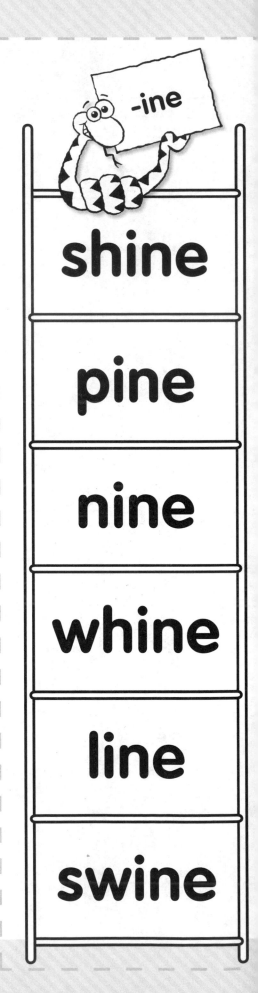

shine

pine

nine

whine

line

swine

CALLER'S CHART

ding	ring	sing	wing
bring	cling	sling	spring
sting	string	swing	thing

CALLER'S CARDS

ding	ring	sing	wing
bring	cling	sling	spring
sting	string	swing	thing

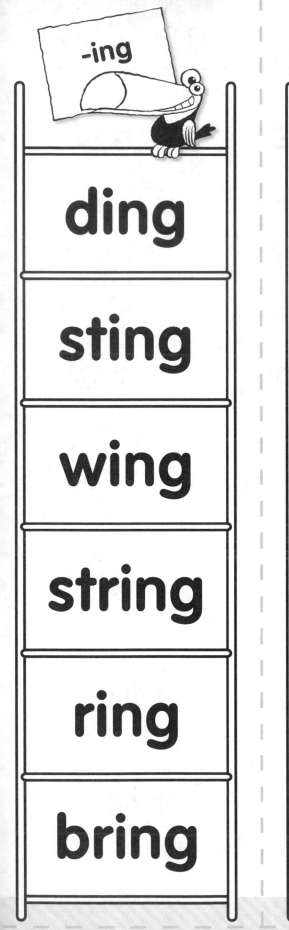

ding
sting
wing
string
ring
bring

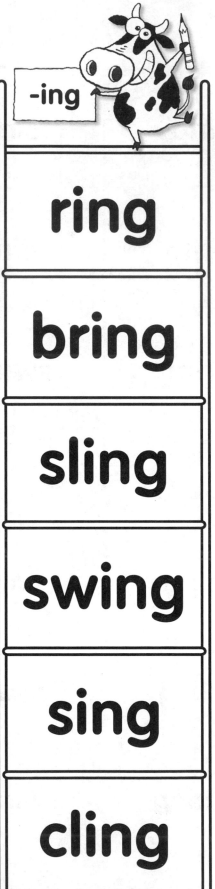

ring
bring
sling
swing
sing
cling

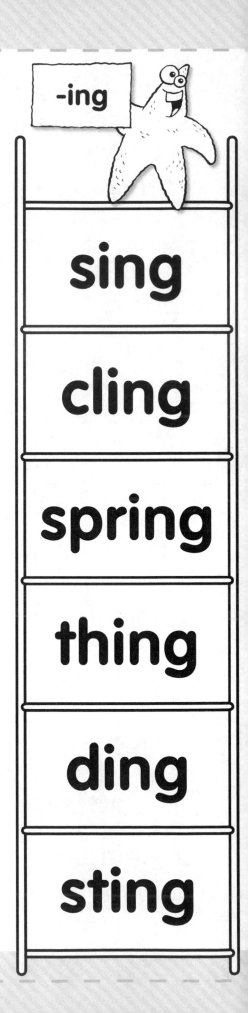

sing
cling
spring
thing
ding
sting

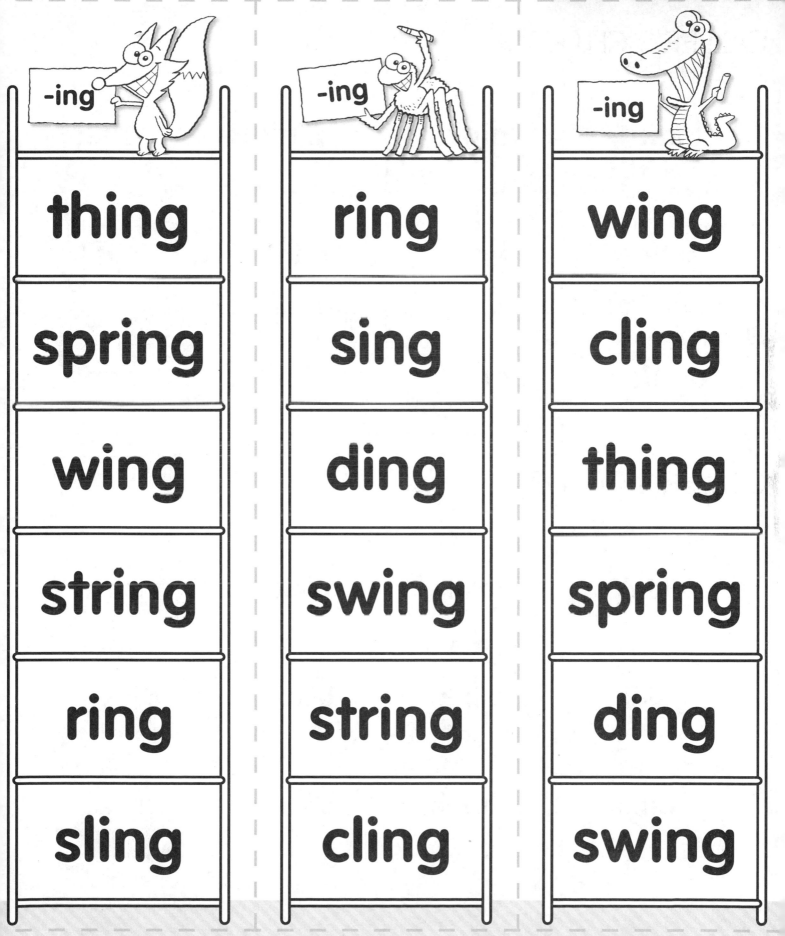

-ing	-ing	-ing
thing	ring	wing
spring	sing	cling
wing	ding	thing
string	swing	spring
ring	string	ding
sling	cling	swing

-ink Family

CALLER'S CHART

kink	mink	pink	rink
sink	wink	blink	clink
drink	shrink	stink	think

CALLER'S CARDS

kink	mink	pink	rink
sink	wink	blink	clink
drink	shrink	stink	think

-ink Family

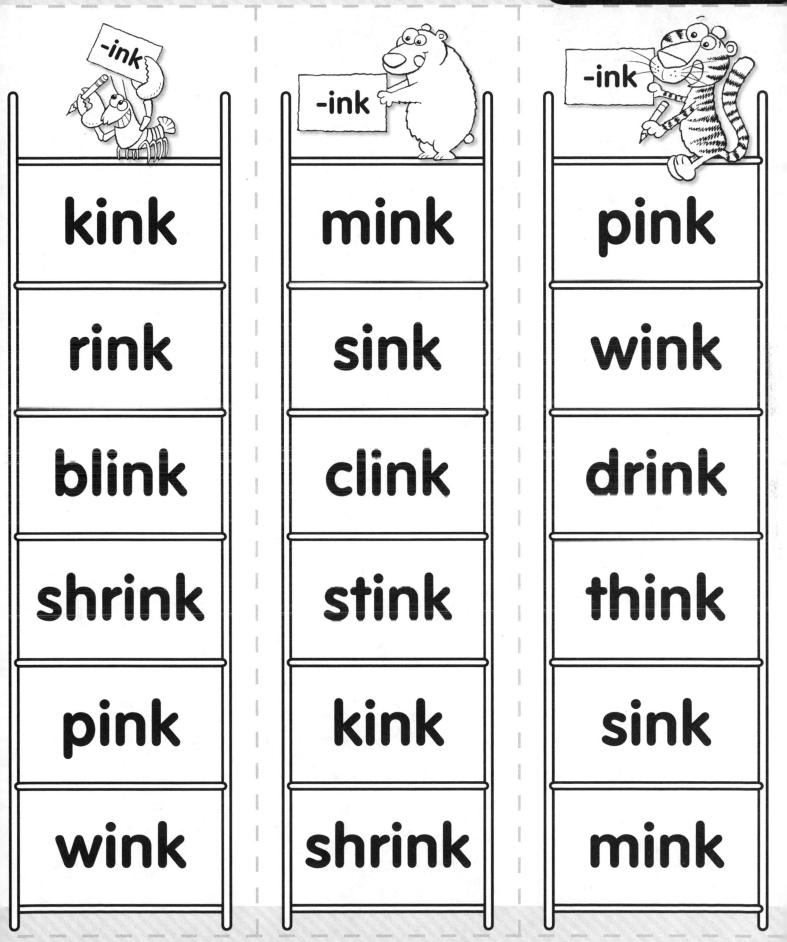

kink	mink	pink
rink	sink	wink
blink	clink	drink
shrink	stink	think
pink	kink	sink
wink	shrink	mink

-ink Family   LADDERS

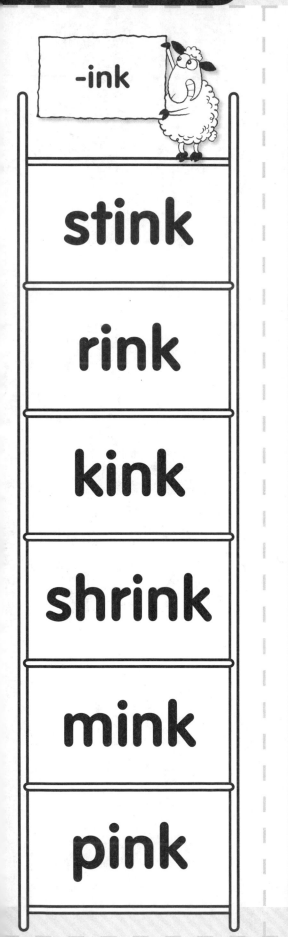

-ink

stink

rink

kink

shrink

mink

pink

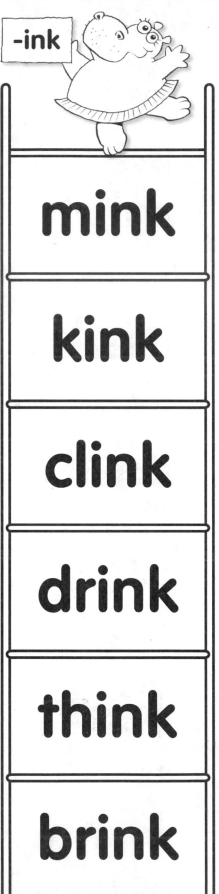

-ink

mink

kink

clink

drink

think

brink

-ink

sink

rink

drink

stink

mink

think

CALLER'S CHART

dip	hip	lip	rip
sip	chip	drip	flip
grip	ship	skip	trip

CALLER'S CARDS

dip	hip	lip	rip
sip	chip	drip	flip
grip	ship	skip	trip

hip	lip	rip
dip	trip	sip
skip	chip	drip
flip	grip	ship
lip	rip	hip
trip	sip	dip

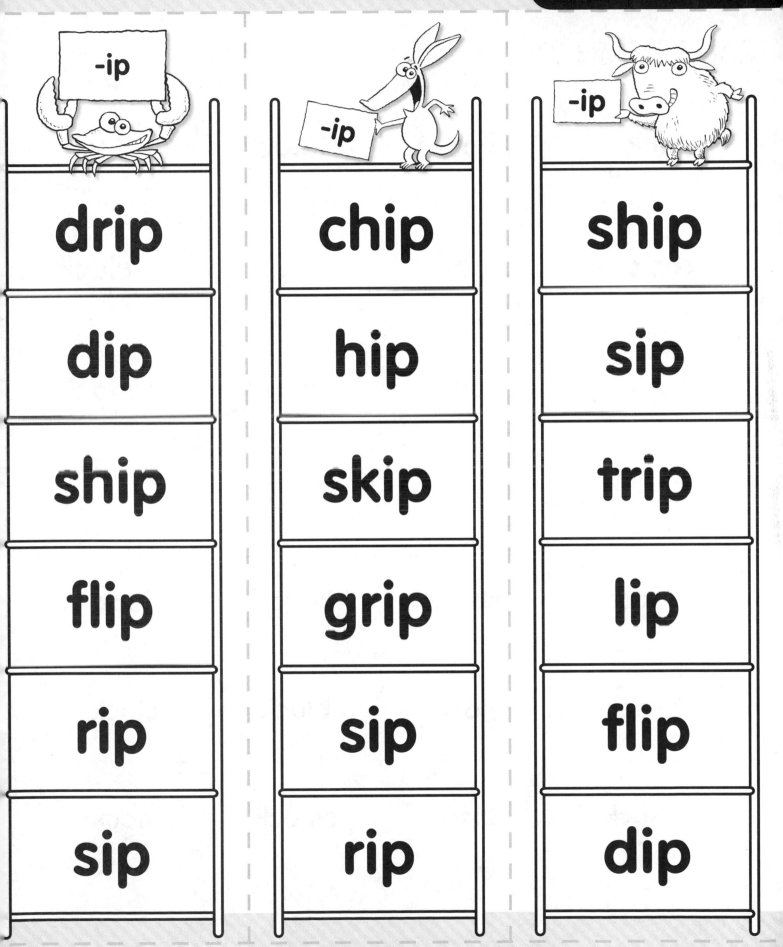

-ip	-ip	-ip
drip	chip	ship
dip	hip	sip
ship	skip	trip
flip	grip	lip
rip	sip	flip
sip	rip	dip

-ock Family

CALLER'S CHART

dock	shock	knock	lock
rock	sock	block	clock
flock	frock	smock	stock

CALLER'S CARDS

dock	shock	knock	lock
rock	sock	block	clock
flock	frock	smock	stock

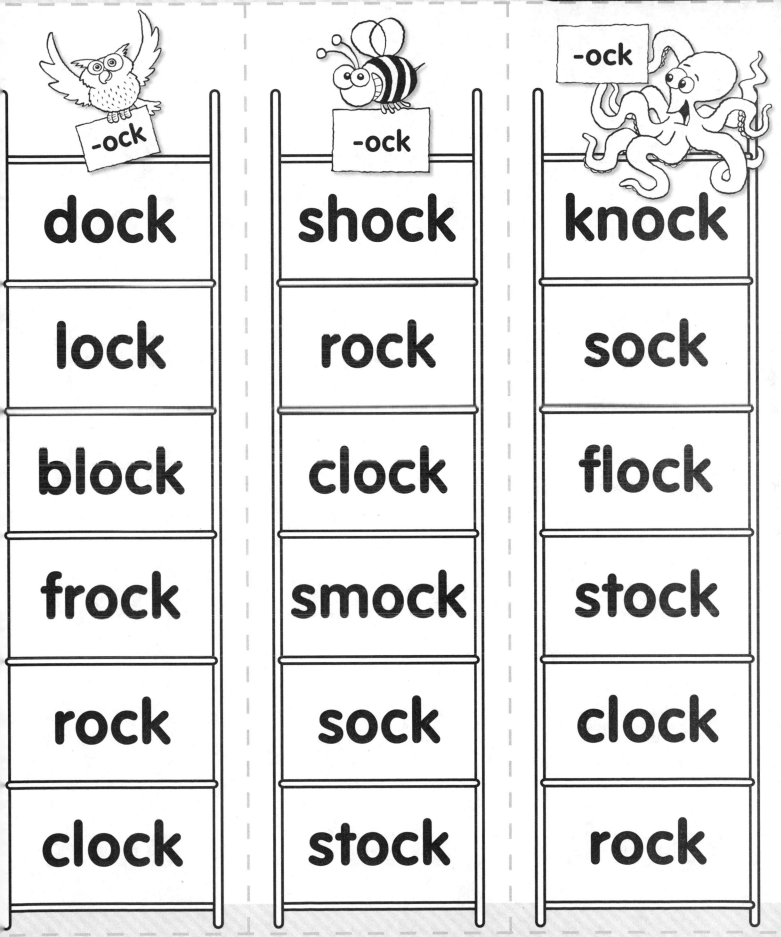

dock	shock	knock
lock	rock	sock
block	clock	flock
frock	smock	stock
rock	sock	clock
clock	stock	rock

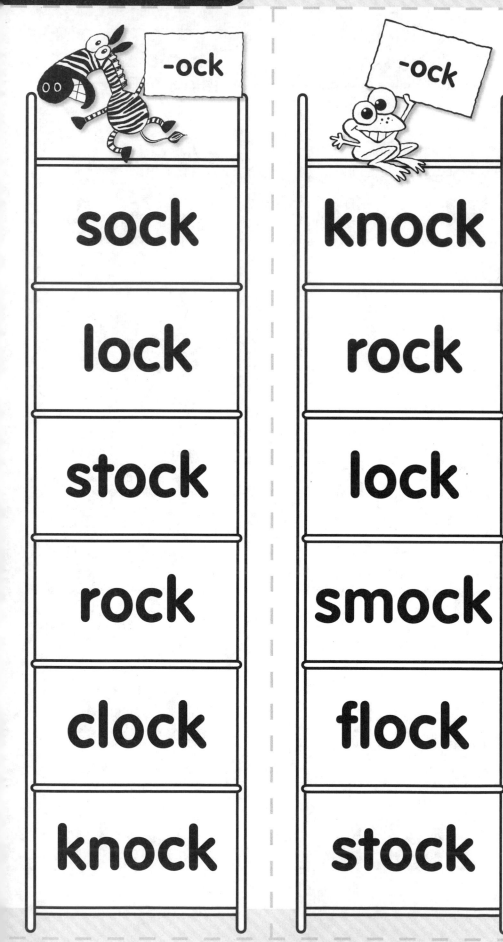

sock	knock	frock
lock	rock	sock
stock	lock	flock
rock	smock	shock
clock	flock	clock
knock	stock	dock

CALLER'S CHART

bore	core	more	pore
sore	tore	wore	chore
score	shore	snore	store

CALLER'S CARDS

bore	core	more	pore
sore	tore	wore	chore
score	shore	snore	store

-ore

-ore

-ore

bore	core	more
pore	sore	tore
wore	chore	score
shore	snore	store
more	bore	core
tore	pore	snore

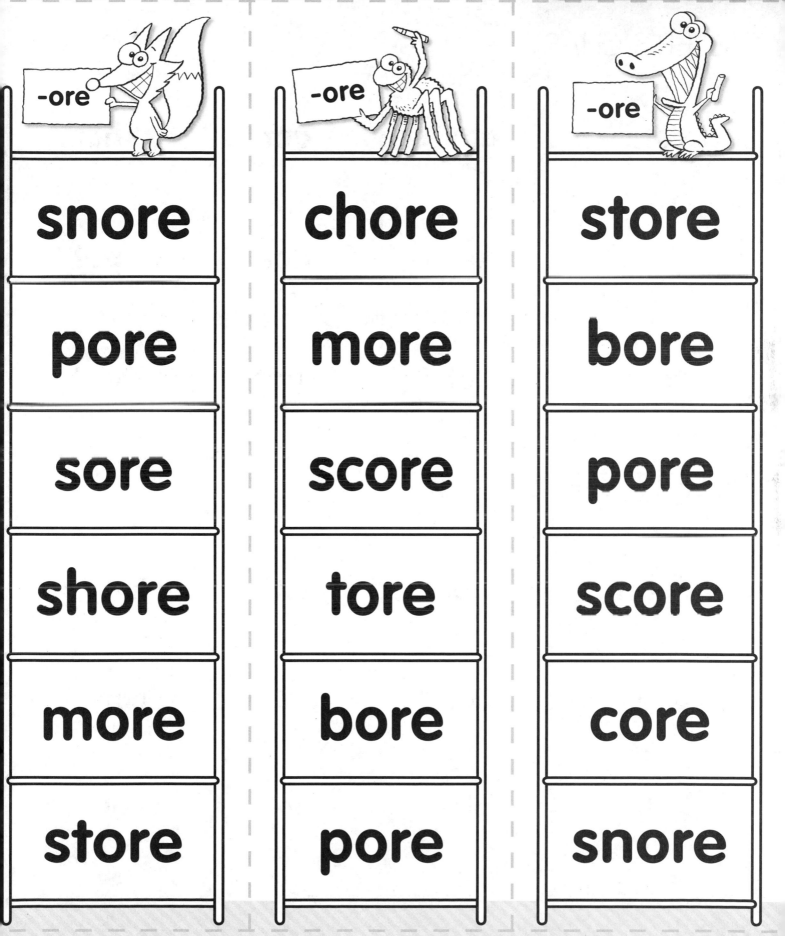

-ore	-ore	-ore
snore	chore	store
pore	more	bore
sore	score	pore
shore	tore	score
more	bore	core
store	pore	snore

CALLER'S CHART

cot	dot	got	hot
jot	lot	not	pot
tot	plot	spot	trot

CALLER'S CARDS

cot	dot	got	hot
jot	lot	not	pot
tot	plot	spot	trot

-ot

-ot

-ot

cot	dot	got
hot	jot	lot
not	pot	tot
plot	spot	trot
dot	got	cot
jot	lot	hot

-ot Family LADDERS

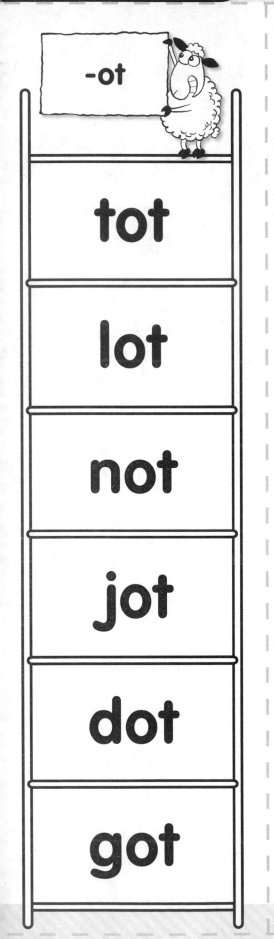

tot	spot	trot
lot	jot	hot
not	pot	cot
jot	plot	trot
dot	got	got
got	dot	not

CALLER'S CHART

buck	duck	luck	muck
puck	suck	tuck	cluck
pluck	stuck	struck	truck

CALLER'S CARDS

buck	duck	luck	muck
puck	suck	tuck	cluck
pluck	stuck	struck	truck

-uck Family LADDERS

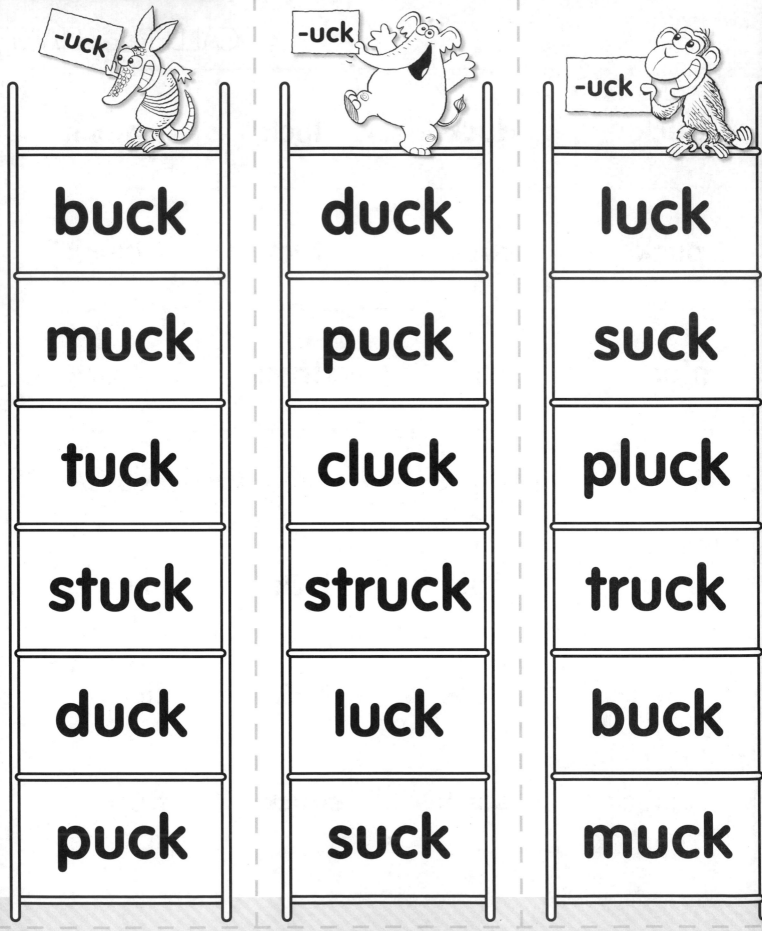

buck	duck	luck
muck	puck	suck
tuck	cluck	pluck
stuck	struck	truck
duck	luck	buck
puck	suck	muck

-uck

cluck

muck

suck

stuck

pluck

puck

-uck

tuck

truck

cluck

struck

buck

suck

-uck

truck

puck

struck

suck

buck

duck

CALLER'S CHART

bug	dug	hug	jug
mug	pug	rug	tug
chug	plug	shrug	snug

CALLER'S CARDS

bug	dug	hug	jug
mug	pug	rug	tug
chug	plug	shrug	snug

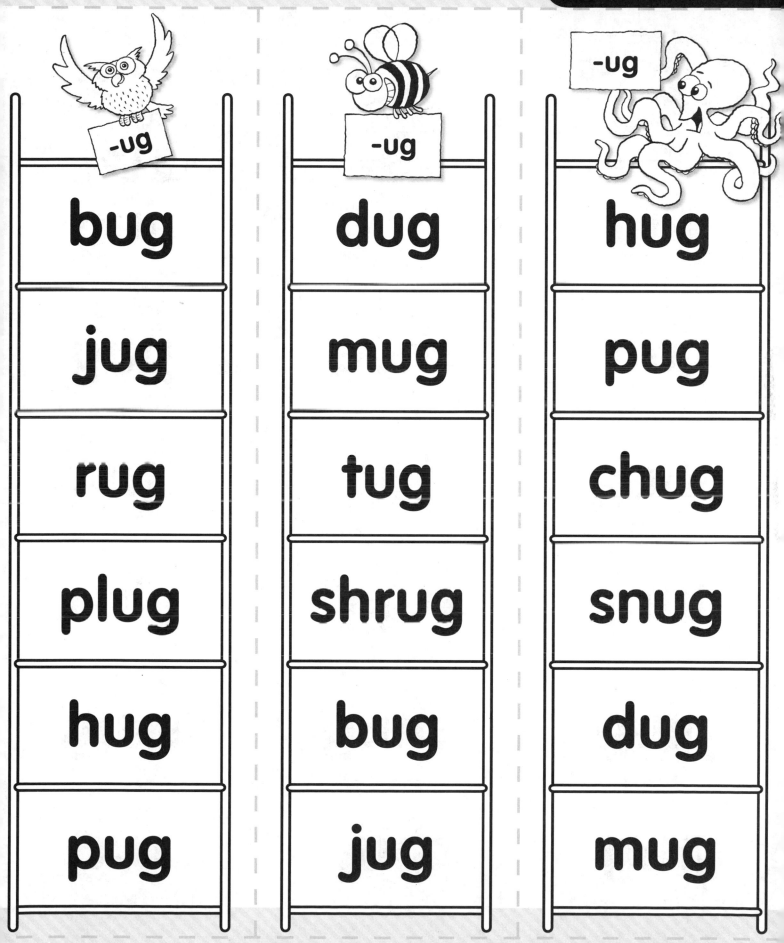

bug	dug	hug
jug	mug	pug
rug	tug	chug
plug	shrug	snug
hug	bug	dug
pug	jug	mug

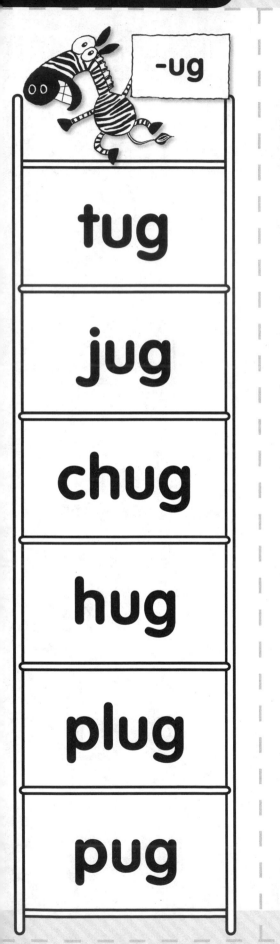

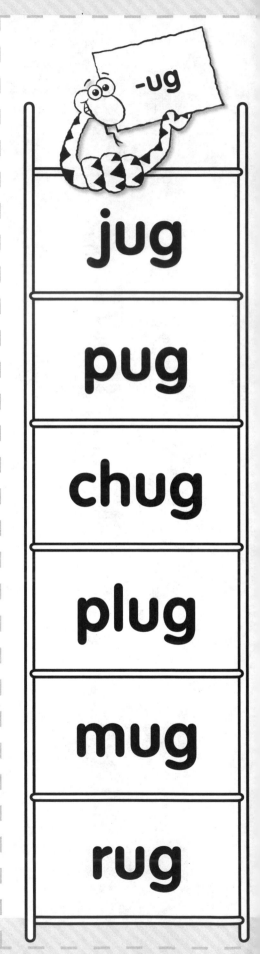

-ug

tug

jug

chug

hug

plug

pug

-ug

pug

mug

tug

rug

snug

chug

-ug

jug

pug

chug

plug

mug

rug

CALLER'S CHART

bump	dump	hump	jump
lump	pump	clump	grump
plump	slump	stump	thump

CALLER'S CARDS

bump	dump	hump	jump
lump	pump	clump	grump
plump	slump	stump	thump

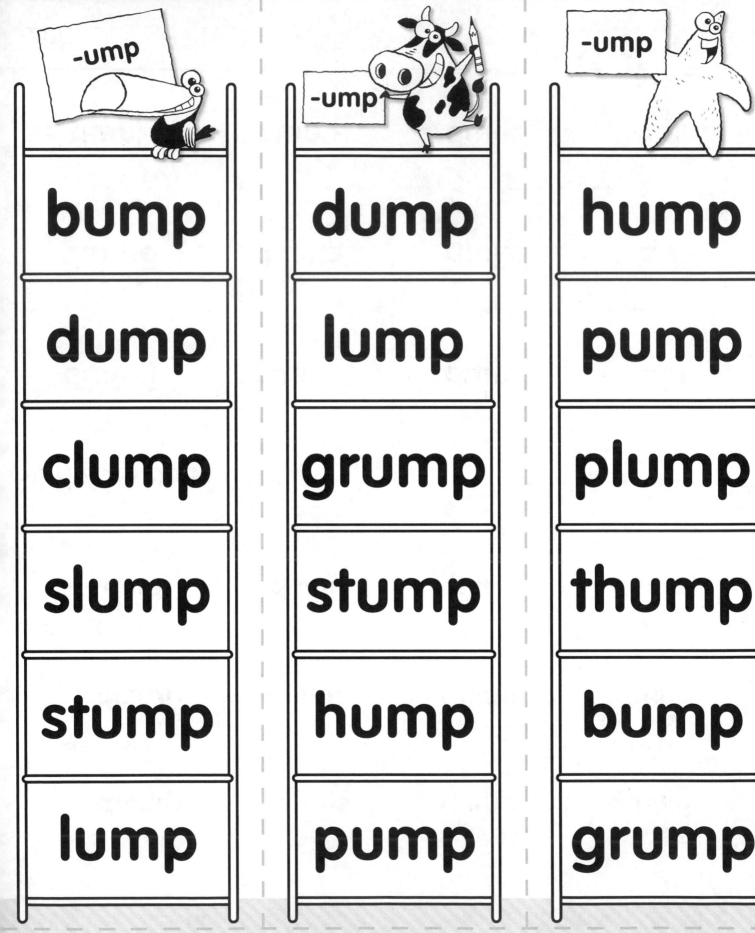

bump	dump	hump
dump	lump	pump
clump	grump	plump
slump	stump	thump
stump	hump	bump
lump	pump	grump

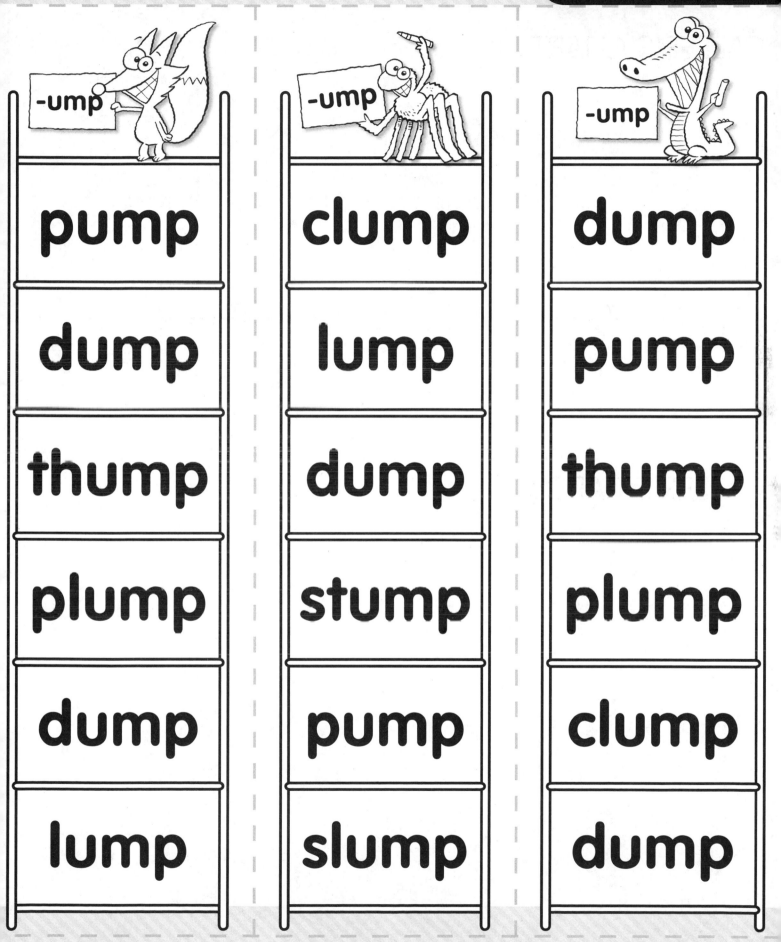

-ump	-ump	-ump
pump	clump	dump
dump	lump	pump
thump	dump	thump
plump	stump	plump
dump	pump	clump
lump	slump	dump

CALLER'S CHART

CALLER'S CARDS

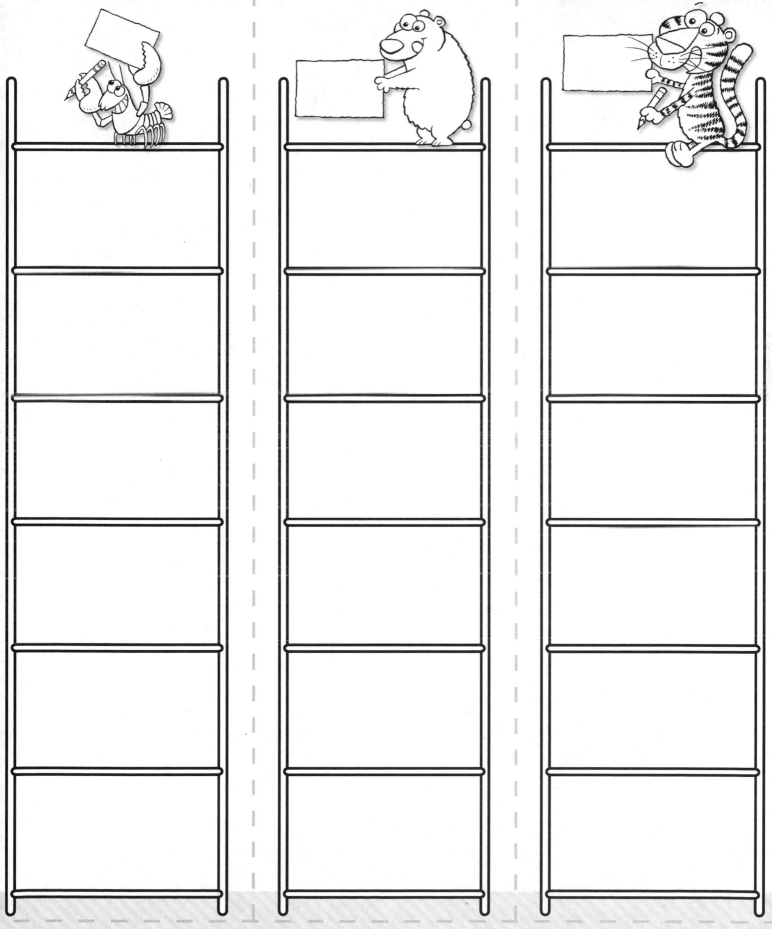

Blank LADDERS

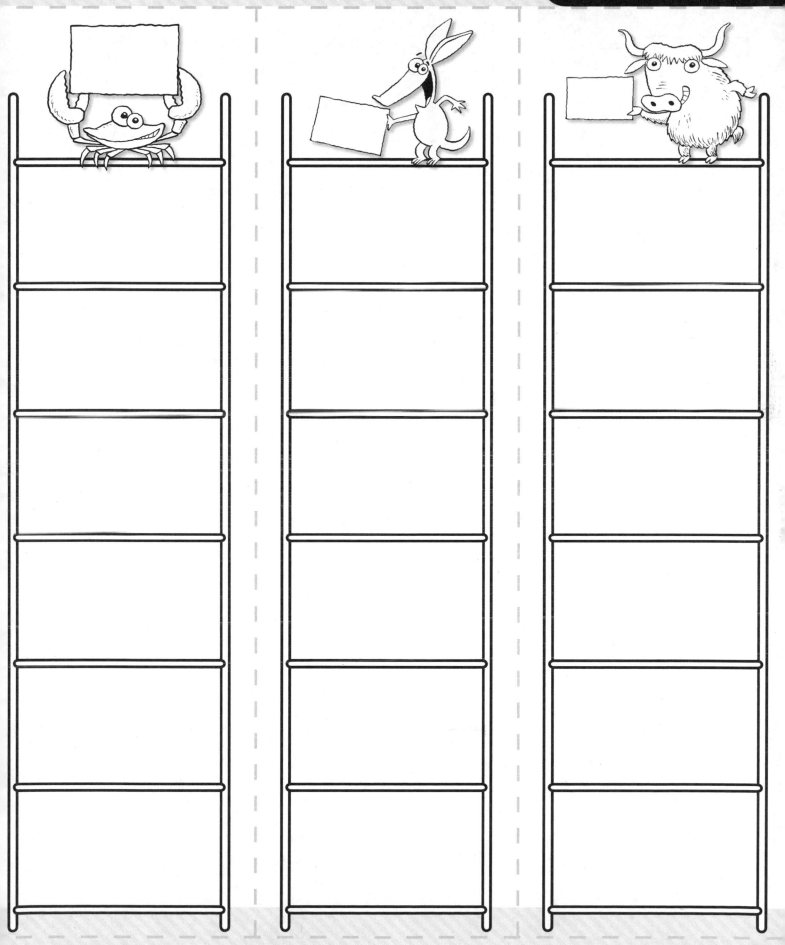

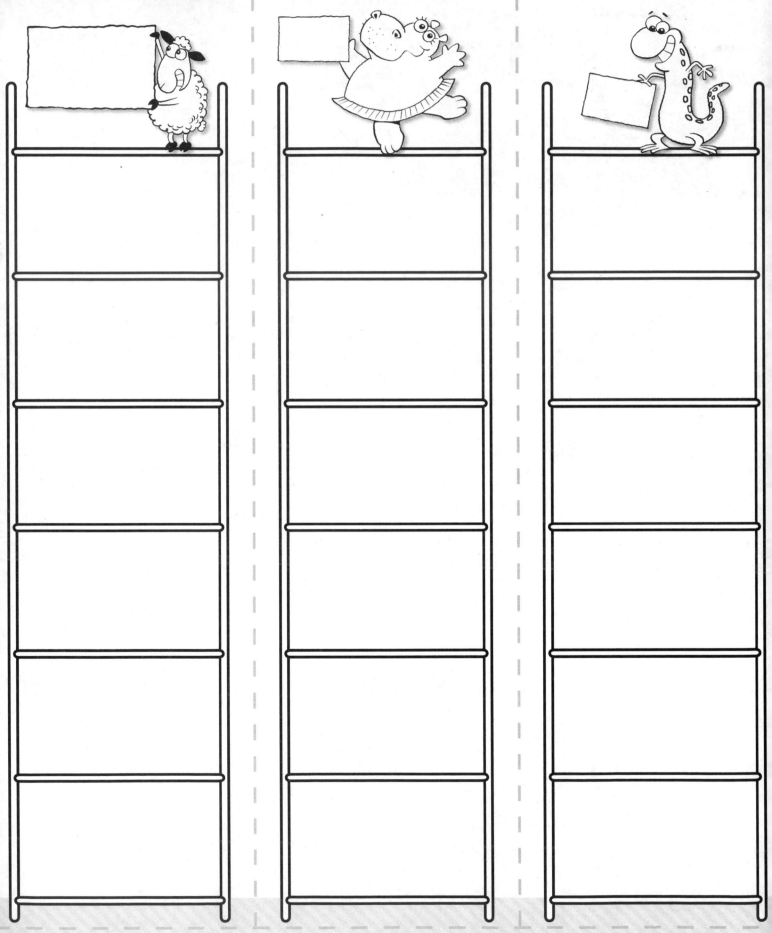

Reproducible Markers (Circles)

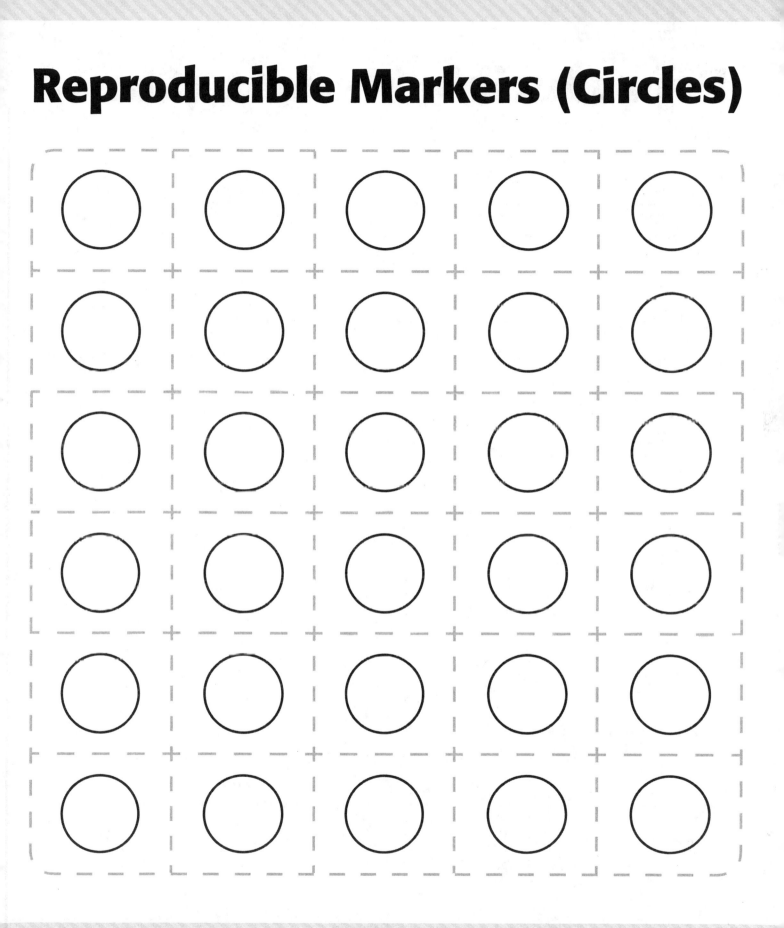

Reproducible Markers (Stars)

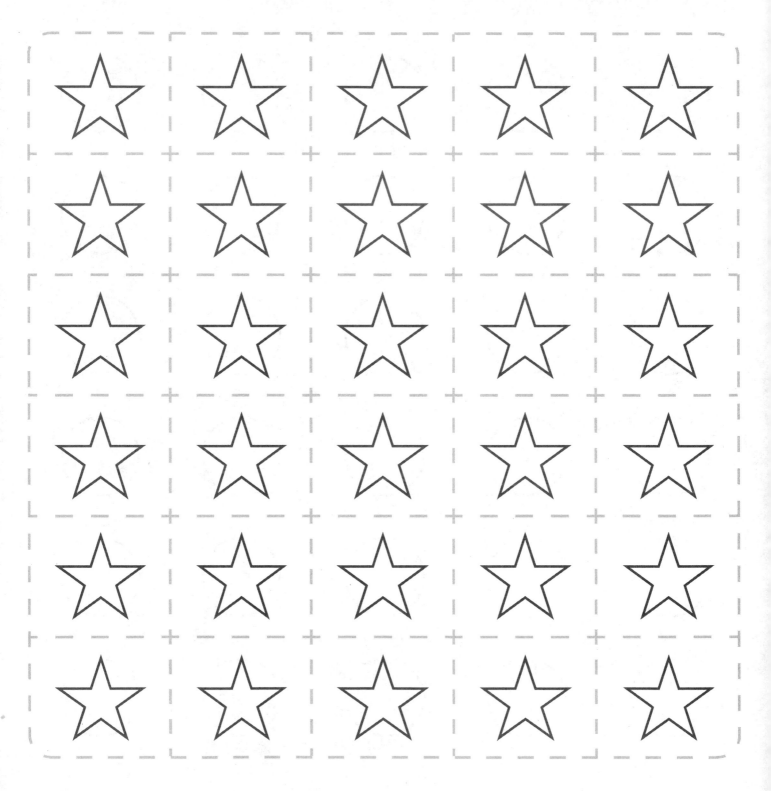

-ump

Word Family Extended Lists

-ack
back
hack
Jack
knack
lack
Mack
pack
quack
rack
sack
tack
lack
black
clack
crack
shack
slack

smack
snack
stack
track
whack

-ail
bail
fail
Gail
hail
jail
nail
pail
quail
rail
sail
tail
wail

flail
frail
snail
trail

-ake
bake
cake
fake
Jake
lake
make
quake
rake
sake
take
wake
brake
drake

flake
shake
snake
stake

-an
ban
can
Dan
fan
Jan
man
Nan
pan
ran
tan
van
bran
clan

plan
scan
span
than

-ank
bank
Hank
lank
rank
sank
tank
yank
blank
clank
crank
drank
flank
Frank

plank
prank
spank
thank

-ap
cap
gap
lap
map
nap
rap
sap
tap
yap
chap
clap
flap
scrap

-ump

93

slap

snap

strap

trap

wrap

-at

bat

cat

fat

gnat

pat

rat

sat

vat

brat

chat

flat

scat

slat

spat

that

-ate

date

fate

gate

hate

Kate

late

mate

rate

crate

plate

skate

state

-eat

beat

feat

heat

meat

neat

peat

seat

bleat

cheat

cleat

pleat

treat

wheat

-ell

bell

cell

dell

fell

jell

Nell

sell

tell

well

yell

dwell

shell

smell

spell

swell

-est

best

jest

lest

nest

pest

test

vest

west

zest

blest

chest

crest

quest

wrest

-y

by

my

cry

dry

fly

fry

pry

shy

sky

sly

spy

try

why

-ick

kick

lick

nick

pick

quick

Rick

sick

tick

wick

brick

chick

click

flick

slick

stick

thick

trick

-ight

fight

knight

light

might

night

right

sight

tight

blight	drill	whine	kink	quip	hock
bright	grill	**-ing**	link	rip	knock
flight	skill	bing	mink	sip	lock
fright	spill	ding	pink	tip	mock
plight	still	ping	rink	zip	rock
slight	thrill	ring	sink	blip	sock
-ill	trill	sing	wink	chip	tock
ill	twill	wing	blink	clip	block
bill	**-ine**	zing	brink	drip	clock
dill	dine	bring	clink	flip	crock
fill	fine	cling	drink	grlp	flock
gill	line	fling	shrink	ship	frock
kill	mine	sling	slink	skip	shock
mill	nine	spring	stink	slip	smock
pill	pine	sting	think	snip	stock
quill	vine	string	**-ip**	strip	**-ore**
sill	shine	swing	dip	trip	bore
till	shrine	thing	hip	whip	core
will	spine	wring	lip	**-ock**	fore
chill	swine	**-ink**	nip	dock	gore

more	not	cluck	snug
pore	pot	pluck	**-ump**
sore	rot	stuck	bump
tore	tot	struck	dump
wore	blot	truck	hump
chore	clot	**-ug**	jump
score	plot	bug	lump
shore	shot	dug	pump
snore	slot	hug	rump
spore	spot	jug	chump
store	trot	mug	clump
swore	**-uck**	pug	frump
-ot	buck	rug	grump
cot	duck	tug	plump
dot	luck	chug	slump
got	muck	drug	stump
hot	puck	plug	thump
jot	suck	shrug	trump
knot	tuck	slug	
lot	chuck	smug	